TEXAS IN TRANSITION

Texas in Transition

Edited by Michael L. Gillette

Lyndon Baines Johnson Library
Lyndon B. Johnson School of Public Affairs

Library of Congress Catalog Card No.: 86-082287
ISBN: 0-89940-419-7

Funding provided by the Lyndon Baines Johnson Foundation

Cover and book design by David Timmons

Cover illustration and illustration p. 140 by Steve Willgren

Photo p. xxx: Old men looking at watches (Russell Lee Collection, Eugene C. Barker Texas History Center).

Photo p. 64: Pennzoil Building (Texas Tourist Development Agency).

CONTENTS

ACKNOWLEDGMENTS

Many of this volume's debts were incurred during the Forum itself. Max Sherman, Harry Middleton, and Paul Burka participated in every facet of the event's planning. William Livingston, Debbie Hanna, William Broyles, Jr., Mike Levy, and Laurey Peat gave valuable advice and support, as did Don Carleton, Liz Carpenter, C. Robert Heath, Jack Keever, Jan Jarboe, Joseph R. Krier, J. Mike Quinn, Martha Smiley, Lyndell Williams, and Terry Young. Moderators of the three panels, George Christian, Joe B. Frantz, and Dave McNeely, gave wise counsel concerning speakers and topics.

Three PBS affiliates, KLRN, KLRU, and KUHT, while planning a television program based on Texas in Transition, helped to shape the event. Tom Spencer, Dick Peterson, Bill Arhos, Howard Gutin, and Jim Bauer were especially helpful in suggesting a new, creative format.

Much of the daily coordination of Texas in Transition as well as the preparation of the manuscript was executed by the LBJ Library's oral history staff. I am grateful to Christie Bourgeois, Gina Gianzero, Ted Gittinger, Joan Kennedy, and Lois Martin for their able and enthusiastic help. Regina Greenwell's dedication to the project and her coordination of a thousand details contributed significantly to the Forum as well as to this publication. The Library's assistant director, Charles Corkran, and Lou Anne Missildine, secretary to the director, oversaw the logistics of Texas in Transition, and underwriting from the LBJ Foundation and the Moody Foundation made both the Forum and its publication possible. Marilyn Duncan, Merry Klonower, and Helen Kenihan of the LBJ School of Public Affairs contributed invaluable help and guidance in transforming the words spoken at the Forum into this published form.

Finally, I would like to thank the following publishers for permitting us to use their material in this volume:

Lines from "Still I Rise," from *And Still I Rise,* by Maya Angelou, copyright 1978, Random House, Inc. Reprinted with permission.

Lines from "The Road Not Taken," by Robert Frost, used with permission of Henry Holt and Company, New York.

Articles by Sam Kinch and Anna Macias reprinted with permission of The Dallas Morning News.

Excerpts from editorial entitled "Texas in Transition," by Bill Neikirk, *Chicago Tribune.* Copyrighted 4/6/86, Chicago Tribune Company, all rights reserved, used with permission.

Article by Mark Singer originally appeared as "Notes and Comment" in *The New Yorker,* May 19, 1986. Reprinted by permission; © 1986, The New Yorker Magazine, Inc.

Article by Felton West originally appeared in *The Houston Post.* Copyright 1986, The Houston Post. Reprinted by permission.

Articles by Greg Curtis, *Texas Monthly Magazine;* Roy J. Eaton, *Wise County Messenger;* Bert Holmes, *The Dallas Times Herald;* Jan Jarboe, *San Antonio Express-News;* Geoffrey Ripps, *The Texas Observer;* Bob Rogers, *Bryan-College Station Eagle;* Kyle Thompson, *Fort Worth Star-Telegram;* Bill Walraven, *Corpus Christi Caller;* Charles Worth Ward, *Wichita Falls Times;* used with permission of the authors and publishers.

Forum panelists, left to right: Alison Cook (back to camera), Diana Hobby, Joe Frantz, Henry Cisneros, Norman Bonner, Larry McMurtry. (Photo by Frank Wolfe, 1986.)

Left to right: Jim Hightower, Earl Lewis, Paul Burka, Dave McNeely, Annette Strauss, Meg Wilson, Bernard Weinstein. (Frank Wolfe, 1986.)

CONTRIBUTORS

T. LOUIS AUSTIN, JR., joined Brown and Root, Incorporated, in 1983 and is presently president and chief executive officer. A graduate of the University of Alabama, he was associated with Texas Utilities in Dallas from 1953 to 1983 and served as chairman and chief executive officer. The various boards on which he serves include the Halliburton Company and the Baptist Foundation of Texas. In 1980 he was the recipient of the John Fritz Medal for outstanding achievement in electrical power generation and leadership in corporate management.

SCOTT BENNETT was born in Decatur, Texas, and educated at Texas Christian University and the University of Texas at Austin. He is a former public affairs editor of *Texas Business* magazine. Mr. Bennett presently lives in Dallas, where he is a management consultant and weekly columnist for the *Dallas Morning News* on business and politics. He is also the business correspondent for *D* magazine.

NORMAN BONNER graduated from the University of Texas at Austin with a B.A. degree in American Studies in

1968. After studying for a year in Chile on a Fulbright exchange grant, he attended Harvard Law School, where he received his J.D. While residing in Fort Worth, Bonner was a recipient of the Earl Warren Fellowship and served as counsel for the NAACP Legal Defense and Educational Fund, Inc. He remained in private practice until 1981 when he became a hearings examiner in the oil and gas division of the Texas Railroad Commission. He is currently an associate with the firm of Akin, Gump, Strauss, Hauer and Feld in Austin and is adjunct professor of law at the University of Texas.

WILLIAM BROYLES, JR., is currently a columnist and contributing editor for *U.S. News & World Report*. He is a graduate of Rice University and Oxford University, where he earned an M.A. as a Marshall scholar. A Marine Corps veteran of Vietnam, he subsequently served as the founding editor of *Texas Monthly*, then editor in chief of *California* magazine and editor of *Newsweek* from 1982 to 1984. He has written numerous articles for these and other national publications, and his book, *Brothers in Arms: A Journey from War to Peace*, was published by Knopf. He has recently moved from New York City to Houston.

PAUL BURKA, *Texas Monthly* senior editor, covers the world of Texas politics for the magazine. Educated at Rice University and the University of Texas School of Law, he is a member of the State Bar of Texas and served as chief counsel to the Texas State Senate Interim Coastal Zone Committee. Burka won the 1985 National Magazine Award for reporting excellence and has also been the recipient of the American Bar Association's Silver Gavel Award and the Texas Institute of Letters' Stanley Walker Award.

GEORGE CHRISTIAN is a political consultant in Austin. His education at the University of Texas led to a career in journalism, during which he was a correspondent for International News Service from 1949 to 1956. He subsequently served as press secretary to Governors Price Daniel and John

Connally. In 1966 he joined President Lyndon Johnson's staff as press secretary and special assistant. His book, *The President Steps Down*, deals with the final year of LBJ's administration.

HENRY CISNEROS has been Mayor of San Antonio since 1981, after having served six years on the City Council. In addition, he has served as executive vice president of the National League of Cities and as a White House fellow, during which time he was an assistant to the secretary of HEW. He is also an educator, having taught at both M.I.T. and the University of Texas at San Antonio. He was educated at Texas A&M University, Harvard University and George Washington University.

ALISON COOK, senior editor of *Texas Monthly*, received her B.A. degree from Rice University in 1970. Before joining *Texas Monthly*, she was a film programmer for the Rice University Media Center, a free-lance writer and senior editor of *Houston City* magazine, as well as hoola-hoop champion of the East Coast, holding a record of eight hours and thirty-six minutes.

JOHN HENRY FAULK is a humorist, author and lecturer on American culture and heritage. He received his education at the University of Texas, taking his B.A. and M.A. in English. He later taught at the University of Texas and was a fellow of the Julius Rosenwald Foundation. He has starred on radio programs, and from 1951 through 1957 he had his own program, "The John Henry Faulk Show" on station WCBS. He has appeared in two movies, *All the Way Home* and *The Best Man*, and authored the book *Fear on Trial*, a memoir of his struggle against McCarthyism. He is a lifelong Texan and currently lives in Austin.

JOE B. FRANTZ, currently Turnbull Professor of History at Corpus Christi State University, recently retired from the University of Texas at Austin after four decades on the history faculty. He served as director of the Texas State Historical Association, 1966-1977, and directed the University of Texas Oral History Project from 1968 to 1974. He also served on the National Park Service advisory board and as a member of the National Historical Publications Commission. Dr. Frantz is the author of many books and articles on Texas and the Southwest, including *Texas, A Bicentennial History* and *The Forty-Acre Follies*.

JIM HIGHTOWER, Texas Commissioner of Agriculture since 1983, is a graduate of North Texas State University. After studying international affairs at Columbia University, he worked for Senator Ralph Yarborough from 1967 to 1969 analyzing agricultural legislation. In 1970 he founded and served as director of the Agribusiness Accountability Project in Washington, D.C. He was the editor of the *Texas Observer* from 1976 to 1979 and is the author of two books.

DIANA HOBBY, a New York native, was educated at Radcliffe College, Georgetown University and, more recently, Rice University, where she is now Associate Editor of Studies in English Literature. Prior to her marriage to Lieutenant Governor Bill Hobby, she taught school and worked as an editor for the U.S. government. Formerly book editor of the *Houston Post*, Ms. Hobby was elevated to membership in the Texas Institute of Letters, in addition to having served as its director. At present she serves on the boards of the Chihuahuan Desert Research Institute in Alpine and St. Johns School in Houston.

MOLLY IVINS is the state political columnist for the *Dallas Times Herald*. A graduate of Smith College, she holds a master's degree from Columbia University School of Journalism and also studied for a year at the Institute of Political Science in Paris. She began her career in journalism in the complaint department of the *Houston Chronicle* and then spent three years as a reporter for the *Minneapolis Tribune*.

In 1970 she returned to Texas as co-editor of the *Texas Observer*, and in 1976 joined the *New York Times*, working as a political reporter. In 1982 she began working for the *Dallas Times Herald*. Ms. Ivins has won numerous journalism awards and in 1976 was named outstanding alumna of the Columbia School of Journalism.

CYNDI TAYLOR KRIER, elected as state senator from Bexar County in 1984, is the first Republican state senator ever elected from the San Antonio metropolitan area and the only woman presently serving in the thirty-one member Senate. She was educated at San Antonio College, Trinity University and the University of Texas at Austin, where she received journalism and law degrees. She served on the White House staff of presidential counselor Anne Armstrong during the Nixon Administration and subsequently as legislative assistant and state office director for U.S. Senator John Tower. In addition to her service in the Texas Senate, Ms. Krier is a member of the Southwest Regional Energy Council and a partner in the law firm of Lang, Cross, Ladon, Boldrick and Green.

EARL LEWIS, currently chairman of the Department of Urban Studies and Brackenridge Distinguished Professor of Urban Studies at Trinity University, received his education from Tougaloo College in Mississippi, Loyola University and the University of Chicago. Dr. Lewis has a special interest in education and has served as a member of the Texas Advisory Commission on the Standards for Duties of School Board Members, and he is currently a member of the Select Committee on Higher Education. He is also a member of the board of the Texas Research and Technology Foundation.

LARRY McMURTRY, a native of Archer City, received his B.A. from North Texas State University and his M.A. from Rice University, where he was a Guggenheim Fellow. A well-known novelist, Mr. McMurty's books include *The Last Picture Show, Horseman, Pass By, Leaving Cheyenne,* and *Terms of Endearment*. His most recent novel, *Lonesome Dove,* won the 1986 Texas Institute of Letters Award for Fiction and the 1986 Pulitzer Prize for Fiction.

DAVE McNEELY was educated at the University of Texas at Austin, where he earned a B.A. degree in journalism and an M.A. degree in government and also was editor of the *Daily Texan,* the student newspaper. He subsequently received an American Political Science Association Congressional Fellowship as well as a Neiman Fellowship at Harvard University. As a journalist McNeely has worked for the *Houston Chronicle,* the *Dallas Morning News,* the *Washington Post,* KERA-TV in Dallas, and since 1978, for the *Austin American-Statesman*. He has hosted or co-hosted statewide television shows about government and politics. McNeely is currently political editor of the *American-Statesman* and writes a column on Texas politics.

BILL MESSER, state representative, attorney and rancher, was educated at Southwest Texas State University and the University of Texas Law School. Before his election to the Texas House in 1978, Messer served as city judge of Belton and City Attorney of Morgan's Point Resort City. Currently he is a partner in the law firm of Messer, Potts and Messer in Belton and is chairman of the Calendars Committee of the Texas House of Representatives and of the Finance Commission of the Texas Legislative Council.

DAVID PRINDLE, a professor of political science at the University of Texas at Austin since 1976, holds a B.A. from the University of California at Santa Cruz, an M.A. from U.C.L.A., and a doctorate in political science from M.I.T. A recipient of the Allan Shivers Teaching Award in 1983, he co-authored *American Politics: The Third Century* and in 1985 edited the *Texas Monthly Political Reader*. He is the author of *Petroleum Politics and the Texas Railroad Commission*.

ANNETTE STRAUSS (Mrs. Theodore H. Strauss) attended Rice University and received her B.A. in sociology from the University of Texas at Austin where she graduated Phi Beta Kappa. She received a master's degree summa cum laude from Columbia University in sociology and psychology. Mrs. Strauss is currently serving her second term as mayor pro tem of the Dallas City Council and is chairman of the National Council of Friends of the Kennedy Center. She is a member of the Development Board of the University of Texas at Dallas and of the Liberal Arts Foundation at the University of Texas at Austin. She has received numerous awards including the prestigious Linz Award for community service. She is currently the director of the Richardson Savings and Loan Association and is a public relations consultant.

BERNARD WEINSTEIN is a graduate of Dartmouth College and Columbia University, where he received his Ph.D. He is currently the director of the Center for Enterprising in the Edwin L. Cox School of Business at Southern Methodist University, as well as professor of finance. Formerly the associate director of the Southern Growth Policies Board, Dr. Weinstein now chairs the Texas Economic Policy Advisory Council.

MEG WILSON, presently science and technology coordinator for the Governor's Office of Economic Development, holds degrees from Ithaca College and the LBJ School of Public Affairs. She entered Texas state government in 1977 in the General Land Office and served there as research associate for the Texas Coastal Management Program and as administrator of Social and Economic Analysis, Environmental Management Division. In 1980 she joined the governor's office, serving as director of policy analysis of the Texas 2000 Long Range Planning Project until 1983. She then served as senior planner in the Governor's Office of Planning and Intergovernmental Relations before assuming her present position.

ABOUT THE EDITOR

A member of the organizing committee for the Texas in Transition forum, Michael L. Gillette holds a doctorate in American history from The University of Texas at Austin. He has authored several articles on the history of the civil rights movement in Texas and since 1974 has headed the oral history program of the Lyndon Baines Johnson Library and Museum.

INTRODUCTION

One hundred fifty years after winning its battle for independence, Texas is engaged in a new struggle. The state that was once a nation has emerged from a dominantly rural entity to a modern urbanized community with new populations, politics, and technologies. Yet in 1986, the industry that has fueled much of this transformation is in trouble. Texas crude oil's price fell from $25 to $13 in ten weeks, sending tremors through the private sector economy and the state and local treasuries. For many Texans the fundamental challenge now is to rally the sagging economy and create a structure for economic development that will prevent similar collapses in the future.

An equally perplexing problem confronted the state even before the current oil crisis. Recognition of the shortcomings and inequities in Texas public education gave momentum to reform, which, in turn, has triggered widespread debate: Have the reform measures been positive? How can they be improved? What revenue measures are necessary if the state is to underwrite quality education?

These dual concerns dominated the thoughts of 220 distinguished Texans who assembled on April 18 to explore their state's heritage and future. Twenty writers, educators, and business and political leaders analyzed the changes of the last fifty years and discussed prescriptions for the future. Joining them was a larger but equally prestigious group who, after listening to the dialogue, then comprised an open forum, weighing in with their own assessments. Texas in Transition: A Sesquicentennial Forum took the place at the Lyndon Baines Johnson Library and Museum in Austin. In addition to the Library, its sponsors were The University of Texas at Austin, *Texas Monthly* magazine, and the Lyndon B. Johnson School of Public Affairs.

The inspiration for Texas in Transition came in the summer of 1985 when *Texas Monthly* announced a forthcoming sesquicentennial issue. The magazine recruited many of the state's most talented authors to write about 150 moments which have shaped modern Texas. News of the upcoming issue led to the proposal: why not assemble these writers and other authorities to extend the magazine's themes through the dynamics of dialogue?

The forum developed from a series of meetings held from September 1985 to March 1986. The planners included Max Sherman, dean of the LBJ School, *Texas Monthly*'s Paul Burka, editor of the sesquicentennial issue, Harry J. Middleton, director of the LBJ Library, and myself. Although we enlarged upon the preliminary concept of a conference of writers and educators to include business and political leaders, the gathering retained its initial character. Its origin caused the forum to be considerably more representative of Texas's professional communicators and observers than of the state as a whole.

This volume presents the forum's dialogue in written form. It also includes a selection of commentaries and published articles written subsequently by forum participants. Although these pages contain the words of Texas in Transition, they cannot adequately transmit the ambience of the event. Word spread on the eve of the forum that Larry McMurtry had won the Pulitzer Prize for his novel *Lone-*

some Dove, and a sense of exhilaration pervaded the entire gathering. In addition, each session had a unique character and atmosphere. Change, Chaos and Culture radiated the powerful inspiration of a fine operatic performance. More evocative of vaudeville than Verdi was the panel on Politics and Economy. A provocative merriment always seems to accompany the philosophical jousting in Texas politics. The panel on The Challenges Ahead was charged with intellectual energy as speakers surveyed problems and solutions for the future. "A town meeting," was *New Yorker* writer Mark Singer's interpretation of the open forum, "characterized by spontaneity, bombast, imaginativeness, pomposity, posturing, heartfelt self-expression—the gamut."

However divergent were the moods, philosophies, and topics of Texas in Transition, one theme recurred with such frequency that it approached consensus: education is the key to the state's economic and cultural advancement. Voice after voice echoed the need for Texas to develop its human infrastructure with policies that are inclusive rather than exclusive. Although Texas has been able to build off the bounty of the earth, as Mayor Henry Cisneros observed, it must now prepare to invest in the bounty of its people. All of its people.

WELCOME

Harry J. Middleton: Texas in its sesquicentennial year is clearly a Texas in Transition from a robust, colorful, adventuresome past to an unknown future. Assembled here today to consider the significance of that is an impressive representation of the state's leading communicators—distinguished authors, journalists, educators, public officials and business leaders.

The genesis of this event dates back to last summer when we first learned that *Texas Monthly* magazine was planning a sesquicentennial issue devoted to critical episodes that made us the way we are. The fact that the magazine was recruiting many of the state's finest writers for this special issue led to the thought: why not amplify this enterprise through the vehicle of a forum—one that we hoped would have statewide proportion—a forum that would ponder those impelling forces of the past and probe for some signs of how our future is to be shaped.

Thus, the Library and the LBJ School of Public Affairs—whose dean, Max Sherman, will preside over this afternoon's session—asked *Texas Monthly* to join in this adventure in which you have been recruited, not only to enrich today's event with your participation, but also with the frank hope that you will be encouraged to extend the dialogue through your own writings and discussions.

We could not have known, even as recently as last summer, how dramatically the oil crisis would reveal the nature of Texas's transition status. On a much happier note, we did not know, however predictable it was, that the Pulitzer Prize committee would add another distinction to our line-up of panelists by awarding that coveted prize to Larry McMurtry for his magnificent novel, *Lonesome Dove.* We are also privileged to have with us Kent Biffle and Robert Compton from another Pulitzer Prize winner—the *Dallas Morning News.*

Although we are calling this a forum and not a symposium, and although unlike our conferences of the past this one plays to an invited and not a general audience, we nonetheless count this as the twentieth in a symposium series which was begun in 1972. Our most faithful participant, one who has attended every one of those events, is with us again today, adding a special distinction to this assembly—Lady Bird Johnson.

Mrs. Johnson, the wildflowers up here are a new touch. They have actually been provided for the benefit of the TV cameras, but I hope it's the start of a tradition and that they will be gracing the tables of symposia here fifty years from now as a continuing reminder of the contributions you have made to the direction, the activities and the spirit of this Library.

As I said earlier, this symposium series began in 1972. We have been most fortunate in having as a co-sponsor from the very beginning the University of Texas. Although special circumstances modified the planning for this one, the planning is usually done by a prestigious committee of University scholars and community leaders. It is another bit of evidence of the special relationship that exists between this Library and the University—a relationship of which we on the Library staff are fiercely proud.

William H. Cunningham: The University of Texas at Austin and the LBJ Library have enjoyed a long and productive relationship. Our cooperative efforts in public education have generated nineteen national symposia, a distinguished lecture series, and scores of publications. The interaction of a national research institution and a major university has enriched each component. For this sesquicentennial forum, we are pleased to welcome a new partner, *Texas Monthly,* and I am proud to note that many of the magazine's fine contributors and executives are graduates of the University. I am pleased to welcome all of you to the campus and to express our appreciation of your participation in this critically important forum.

Jake Pickle: In the nation's Capitol, in the Rotunda high above that center part of the big dome, are the Brumidi friezes, the design of that great artist to show the progress of the United States in increments of approximately every twenty years. A very moving scene, if you've been there in the Capitol. We finally finished it in the early fifties after almost a hundred years' work. And then we stopped; we haven't put another frieze on the wall to show our progress. The reason is the world is moving too fast. We simply cannot pause long enough even to evaluate the progress and the happenings.

During this space of almost one generation, or a half, we've seen the atom bomb, television, a walk on the moon, and the computers, all of which definitely affect the lives of every person in the world and certainly in the United States. We've stopped the friezes. We've moved at such an accelerated and technical rate that we can't even pause long enough to record the changes. The national changes are there, and the states are making these same kinds of changes.

Texas has made probably more progress than any other state in the Union. My northern colleagues would say it was because we had further to go. The fact of the matter is that

Texas is the pre-eminent state of the Union today. The Sun Belt is more a fact than a phrase. We have made great progress, and yet we are going to be affected by many factors that face the United States citizen today—factors and problems that relate to the deficit, that relate to our leadership in the free world, the way in which we handle our immigration to maintain our status as the melting pot of the world, our own financing system of fiscal responsibility. And can we actually continue to finance our government through the income tax alone? These are problems that face us, and they are going to affect every state. I am confident, though, that we're going to handle them, and that this state is going to do it and going to do it in as good a shape as anybody. I'm confident because, one, oil and gas will come back. I'm confident of that. Second, the South will rise; it has already risen. And third, I look forward to the fact that Jim Wright is going to be our next speaker; that won't hurt our state at all. There's a possibility that our senator, Lloyd Bentsen, will be the chairman of the Finance Committee. Down the line you could even have a chairman of the Ways and Means Committee from Texas. These things won't hurt our state at all.

Now we're in a state of transition and I think our citizens are kind of nervous and impatient. We want to get on with it. We like to walk tall and talk big. That's our nature and we're going to continue to do it. But we also are realistic. So in conclusion I compliment the people who are going to put this forum on. I welcome all the people here for this think tank session.

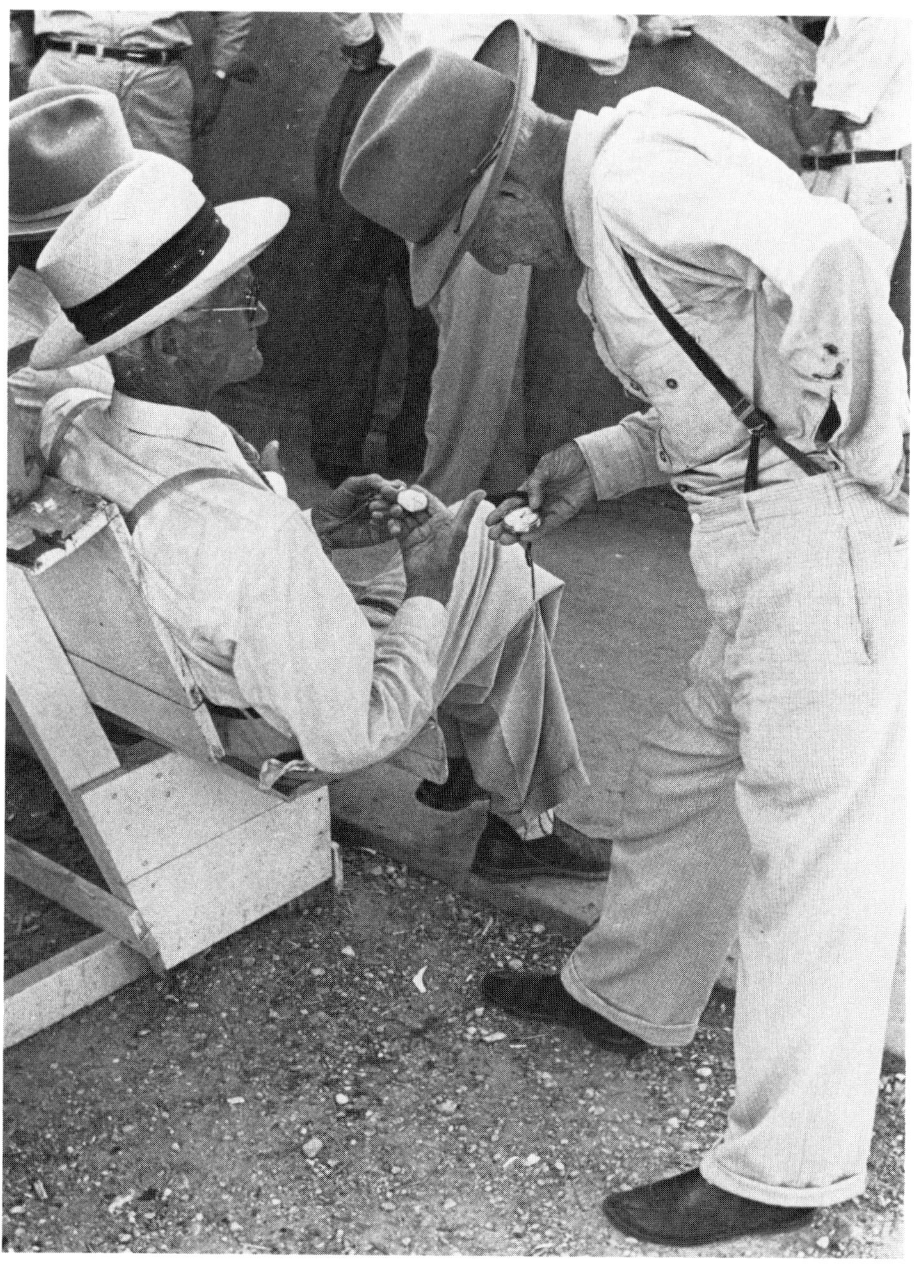

THE MAKING OF MODERN TEXAS

CHANGE, CHAOS AND CULTURE

Joe B. Frantz: I'm going to chair this panel with as little visibility as possible. I found my metier in life about twenty years ago when I was privileged to share a cab with Luci Johnson from LaGuardia to downtown New York. The taxi driver, like all New York taxi drivers, who make a point of knowing every celebrity, recognized Luci. He talked her arm off all the way, once in a while letting her say something. He finally let her out at her hotel and then he turned to me and he said, "Where are you going?" And I told him. We drove a half a block, he turned around and he said to me, "You're not anybody important, are you?" Since then I've known where I stood.

In 1914 Jim Ferguson, who was one of the great names, if not great men—that's debatable—of Texas twentieth-century history, opened his campaign for governor at Mount Calm, Texas, which was a village then and is a village now. Over the next several months he made dozens, even hundreds, of campaign speeches. Only three of them were in what we would call metropolitan centers. One reason was we didn't have much in the way of metropolitan centers. The other was that Texas was an agricultural state. Jim was running as the farmer's friend, and that's what got you into office. So he just ignored the city vote. As late as the beginning of World War II, we were still a heavily rural-oriented state. Even the people who had moved to town had remained country in their thinking. World War II bounced us out of all of that. The changes since 1945, or even since 1941, have been both demonstrable and at times dizzying.

So it's quite right that we're here today to talk about what was, what is, what may be, and we're going to deal with the change right now and the chaos that's come with it. Chaos, of course, is welcome. We would like an orderly world. For that matter, so would the Soviets. On the other hand, this may be the most interesting time in which to be living since the Catholic church and the Protestants went at each other a half-millennium ago. These are the times when we don't know where we're going, but we do get the feeling we're going somewhere else. And Texas, which is not really a member of the United States but an affiliate, is going along with it. So we're here to assay where we've been and where we're going.

Now, this is a sesquicentennial and I think we ought to raise the question: a hundred and fifty years of what? Basically we're celebrating a hundred and fifty years of Anglo-American domination of the area and we are ignoring the fact that we go back four hundred and fifty-eight years, mildly, to the beginning of the Spanish occupation, exploration of this area, and that the Spanish gave us a tremendous heritage. We don't brag about it, but we should: the first state with community property laws, the first state with a homestead act, the first state to give illegitimate and adoptive children equal rights, the first state to say that water belonged to all the people and not to those who had the money. These are just a few things in our Spanish heritage that we should not ignore in this hundred and fifty years of celebration of the Texas Declaration of Independence against Mexico. This heritage also gave us a feeling of amplitude, of spaciousness, which has never left us and which, regardless of our origins, has infected our spirit.

Texans do have a certain nationalism about them that you don't find in other states. In fact, I find the other states quite parochial despite all their presumed cosmopolitanism. J.

Frank Dobie had an international reputation as a folklorist. When he died, the *New York Times* noted it duly, referring to him as "a well-known Texas humorist." We're all funny, we're yahoos, we talk differently, we think differently, we're loud, and we do brag frequently about the wrong things. I won't go into that. They have accused Larry McMurtry of being a regional writer, which is like saying Jesus was a regional person; he never got far from Jerusalem or Nazareth. Author William Faulkner stayed in his own county for a lifetime and therefore was strictly a one-county Mississippi writer. Truth is wherever you find it, experience is wherever you find it. And you don't have to go far from home to find it. So here we are then, a people who would like to be recognized, who would like to be loved and who are at the same time contentious, prickly, and I think, without being at all nationalistic, something to be proud of.

I'll close my short statement with a fact some of you football fans will remember. When SMU was in its glory days with Kyle Rote, they played Notre Dame up in Dallas in one of the all-time great southwestern football games. There was a priest in the stands who was beating on everybody within reach saying, "Come on, Mustangs! Come on, Rote!" Finally one of his churchmen challenged him and said, "That's Notre Dame they're playing out there." He said, "Yes, I'm a Catholic priest, but I am a Texan first." So that's where we are now.

Larry McMurtry is the most recent Pulitzer Prize winner. His is basically our state's first in literature, although Katherine Anne Porter got one. Whether she was a Texan is debatable, but she did come from here. She never liked Texas, and Texans never read her. They have read Larry. But there's one thing about Larry which is going to make him unique and I feel that uniqueness will remain: he probably is the only Pulitzer Prize winner in literature who ever heard the news in Uvalde.

Larry McMurtry: I have to tell one brief Pulitzer Prize story to illustrate the effervescent nature of fame, so you won't think I'm taking myself too seriously. I drove into Uvalde on Wednesday night to make a speech at the junior college there, and the Holiday Inn graciously put my name on the marquee. When I drove in, I saw a little sign saying, "Welcome, Larry McMurtry, author of *Terms of Endearment.*" That's not the funny part of the story. I thought that was wonderful. I've spent about a hundred nights a year in Holiday Inns and have written most of my books in them and certainly wrote most of *Lonesome Dove* in them. And I thought that was quite a nice accolade.

I got up the next morning and did my duty and spoke for around six straight hours to the citizens of Uvalde and the students of the college. I went back to my room, hoping to take a brief nap before I resumed my lecturing duties. The news came that I had won this great honor. I walked over to the lobby to meet the first representative of the press. As I was walking into the lobby, I happened to notice that they were scraping my name off the marquee and putting up "Lunch Special—Catfish $3.59."

I've been on a lecture tour around the state in the past ten days, lecturing largely at junior colleges, community colleges, state teachers colleges. I feel like I've been speaking for a hundred and fifty years. And as I was driving around, knowing that I was going to end my little tour with this assembly, I tried to think about Texas and its birthday. I reflected first that in fact the state as a state is only a hundred years older than I am. I myself have seen a third of its history. If you contrast this with cities in China, certain cities that have been inhabited continuously for six thousand years, it seems like a very short time. What could one say? What should one say? What qualities should one look for in a place that has been existing as an entity for a hundred and fifty years?

I think what so far has distinguished Texas is its energies. I'm not talking about the petroleum industry, either. I'm talking about its human industries, which actually in a rather shorter period of time than that, almost in my lifetime, has turned Texas from a rural and agricultural state into an urban entity. Energy is a quality that's not spoken about much, but it should never be underestimated. It should be applauded, because I think that sheer raw energy is a central part of the DNA of achievement. Without it, there isn't going to be much achievement. But energy alone won't give you a considered culture, the kind of culture that some of these older places have and that I think that we want and need in Texas. In my little tour I've had the experience of simply trying to drive through each of the major cities in Texas. That has made me wish for a more considered culture that would build freeway systems faster. Because if we don't consider certain aspects such as mass transit, what we're going to have is an urban gridlock all over the state. It is remarkably difficult to get through any of our cities now.

I reflected about this assembly all week. I believe as a writer I have probably spoken at more of the really small schools in the state than any other Texas writer. I've spoken at every community college in the Dallas system, I've spoken at most of the state teachers colleges. I've spoken at a goodly number of the junior colleges, just as I was doing yesterday. I'm sure that I have been the first writer, just within the last week, that perhaps a thousand students have ever seen or listened to or shaken hands with. Since I spend my life essentially trying to satisfy the needs of my own imagination, I largely talk to these students about the imagination, about what a fascinating thing it is, about what a rich and satisfying life one can have by attempting to satisfy it, and what a complex experience it is to work entirely with one's own imagination—the experience of life that one's region gives when filtered through one's own imagination. I see a sense of astonishment in the faces of these students. They've never thought of this before.

Texas is a place that's a hundred and fifty years old, a place that is one step from the frontier. Its first concern, and quite properly, has been with survival: with its own survival and with the survival of its families, with the survival of its communities, with the survival of its culture and with its economic survival. We have achieved this now. We're not terribly threatened. The transition that I hope to see for Texas is one I've seen the promise of in the response of the students that I've spoken to this past week—the sudden realization that when you make a more dense imaginative experience, a richer, better textured, more complex imaginative experience, you suddenly bring a dimension into life that many of them had just not suspected. I hope that the general movement of educational reform that's afoot in Texas right now will fulfill this promise for the next generations of students and young people in Texas. I think we'll have a much richer and more satisfying culture as a result.

Alison Cook: It was not my intention originally to talk about oil today, but it's a funny thing about twentieth-century Texas. Oil has a way of seeping in regardless. No matter where you turn, you end up as viscous and gooey as James Dean in *Giant.* You all remember the scene: "Boy meets gusher," the perfect Texas romance, Lord help us.

That black stuff has fueled enormous changes in Texas culture over the past fifty years. Oil gave us our cities, or rather induced us to create our cities in the shape we know them, starting in the forties—really, perhaps even earlier with the great East Texas strikes of the thirties. Oil lured Texans out of the countryside. It lured outsiders into the state, and by 1960 three-quarters of the population was urban. Oil booted Texas into an automobile culture that shaped those cities physically and also replaced the horse culture in our hearts and minds. Oil and gas taxes provided the flood of public funds that paid for our outrageously good road system that bound us all together until Southwest Airlines came along to bind us even better.

But, most of all, oil gave us the wherewithal to catch up with the rest of the country. Suddenly there was a lot of new wealth in Texas. In the sense of culture, in its narrow arts-and-letters definition, that was a pretty good thing for Texas. Rich Texans got busy funding museums and symphonies and grand operas and theaters and ballet companies. So what if the culture they were importing wasn't indigenous? You had to start somewhere. And so what, really, if there wasn't much in Texans' broader culture—which was a pragmatic and action-oriented system of values and attitudes if there ever were one—that would really have dictated support for the arts? New American money has, since time began, bought status and bought respectability through good cultural works. New Texas money was no exception.

Some of the early results were less than wonderful, though. For years Houston's Museum of Fine Arts felt obliged to cater to rich and very demanding patrons who had generously donated rather mediocre collections. One apocryphal Houston tale holds that oilman Hugh Roy Cullen agreed to fund the Houston Symphony handsomely on condition that they play "Old Black Joe" for him at concerts. I won't vouch for the absolute authenticity of that tale, but it's exactly the sort of thing that's spawned the modern Texas social disease that a friend of mine, the writer Nick Lemann, calls rubophobia, the inordinate fear of being taken for a rube, a yahoo, an easily caricatured figure of fun.

Oil gave us rubophobia, of course. The feared and hated object of this syndrome was precisely the new Texas stereotype created by the petroleum boom: the vulgar, ostentatious Texas oilman, the millionaire with too much money for his own good. He's the guy chronicled at such excruciating length in *New Yorker* writer John Bainbridge's *The Super Americans.* Bainbridge gave most of the rest of the world ample cause to think that all of Texas had just fallen off a very large turnip truck. The publication of the book in 1961 made rubophobia into a minor Texas epidemic. The interesting thing about rubophobia, though, is that as as a cultural strain it flies right in the face of what is popularly supposed to be Texans' great self-assurance, our legendary freedom from self-doubt, a legacy, we are told, from our successful subordination of the frontier. But of course by the sixties there were generations of urban Texans that had been far removed from the struggles of the frontier. Whatever the cause, rubophobes felt free to indulge in a little colonial insecurity.

But being Texans, they also did something about it: they gave with a vengeance. Rubophobia put a nice extra spin on fund-raising born of either a sincere passion for the arts or even a yen for social climbing. As a result, Texans ended up with some really good stuff: the Grand Opera in Houston, the Kimbell Museum in Fort Worth, respectable regional theaters are all things that come to mind. We acquired some mighty fine temples of commerce from modern Medici developer princes like Gerald Hines, who in a sort of subtle rubophobia resolved that their Texas skyscrapers would be second to none. If any of the above cultural wonders got certified by the *New York Times,* why, so much the better. All good Texas rubophobes would celebrate.

The worrisome side of rubophobia, I think, though, is that at heart it wants to make Texas less like itself and more like everywhere else. Take liquor-by-the-drink, a cherished rubophobe cause that really has changed the face of Texas, if you think about it. Rubophobes represented a new generation of Texans who wouldn't be caught dead clutching a brown paper sack with a bottle of liquor in it. No glass, no class. And besides, all those brand-new Texans who had been flocking in to the burgeoning oil economy would never buy our eccentric liquor laws. Furthermore, we couldn't get the convention and tourist business that we needed. So eventually liquor-by-the-drink came to pass. And so did the relentless upscaling of Texas. Liquor sales gave all those expensive hotels and restaurants the profit margins they needed, and they bred like prairie dogs. Even the legislature went upscale; they deserted the time-honored trees of scruffy old Scholz's beer garden for the vastly cushier Quorum. The Quorum was on top of the bank, and the Quorum could have been anywhere.

If, as T. R. Fehrenbach has suggested, the history of Texas as Texas will end the moment we lose all our mythology, and the moment that the office-working, car-driving Texan, as he puts it, is completely indistinguishable from his northern counterpart, I guarantee you that rubophobia and liquor-by-the-drink will be more than a little to blame.

But I prefer to think that the history of Texas as Texas will persist as long as we keep our sense that the world isn't finished yet. That's what drew me instinctively to the state when I arrived here from Vermont twenty-one years ago: the pervasive feeling that nothing has been decided yet. I still feel that, driving the streets of Dallas and Houston and Austin and San Antonio. The evidence is there to read, that the 1965 immigration reform that abolished those quotas on non-Europeans has ended up combining with the frenetic oil boom of the late seventies and early eighties to change the state's cultural profile in a way we don't even understand yet. I can see it in the startling Chinese commercial center that covers almost all of old downtown Richardson, of all places. And I can see it in the bustling commerce of Houston's Little Saigon, in the Indochinese ghetto of East Dallas. I can see it in the sari stores that dot all of Southwest Houston, in the Nigerian cabbies that are lined up at Hobby Airport, in the new immigrant housing, those fifteen-year-old apartment complexes in Houston and Dallas that are now home to thousands of recent arrivals from Asia and from Central and South America.

That oil-driven boom brought them, and I think the bust will take some of them away, but many of them do seem here to stay. When I read about some Indochinese kid graduating at the top of his class, and when I find out that the most talented cook at my favorite Thai restaurant in Houston is a twenty-year-old Mexican-American from McAllen, then I think that Texas is still in the process of inventing itself, and I think that anything could happen here. That, in Texas mythology, has always been the point.

Norman Bonner: This is a peculiarly appropriate topic, since the civil rights movement has been blamed for a lot of the change and chaos that the state has seen. Rightly or wrongly it has received the credit or blame.

With regard to culture, however, a fleeting retrospective is in order here. First of all, black Texans have been a part of Texas's landscape even before there was a Texas. Plaques bearing ancient Libyan writing have been found in the Big Bend. These were discovered by archeologists in the early sixties. So apparently some black Texans came here before Columbus.

In the middle eighteenth century a Spanish colonizer named Jose de Escandon came upon a black Indian tribe near the mouth of the Rio Grande. Unlike other tribes, these "Indians" had Negroid features and fought with shields and spears. They are thought to have escaped from a wrecked slave ship or from a slave colony on a nearby island.

Civil rights as an issue actually had its genesis in the Republic of Texas, where many black Texans were free and lived among their Anglo brothers. Such black Texans served in the Texas Revolution. Many of those soldiers were rewarded with land grants. As the Republic of Texas developed, efforts were launched to squeeze some of the free blacks out of the state. Sam Houston, the first president of the Republic, resisted a number of these efforts by liberally granting exemptions to those free blacks to remain in the state.

The post-Reconstruction era, of course, is where the civil rights movement really has its genesis or its origins in the state, as efforts were made by the newly empowered, retrograde elements of the post-Reconstruction South to disenfranchise black citizens and to deny them the benefits of education. Indeed it was in these two areas that all of the subsequent major battles were fought, that is in the areas of education and voting rights. The white primary is a perfect example. It dates back to 1874, when enactments were promulgated to restrict access to the Democratic Party primary. However, as bleak as that period was, it was not without rays of hope. The first women's strike in Texas apparently took place in Galveston and was staged by black laundry workers who were seeking better working conditions and higher wages. This occurred in 1872.

Black voters in certain limited numbers were able to participate in the post-Reconstruction electoral process until the enactment of the poll tax in 1902, which drastically reduced the number of people who could afford to vote, blacks and whites. It had a devastating effect on black participation in the electoral process. Scholars report that with the poll tax, the number of black voters who were able to participate in Texas elections dropped from approximately one hundred thousand in the 1890s to an estimated five thousand by 1906. At the same time, of course, the NAACP, which later took a very prominent role in enforcing civil rights laws, was formed and came to Texas.

The voting rights issue gathered a full head of steam in 1927 with the Supreme Court decision that began a series of lawsuits between parties seeking to open up the Democratic primary. The state law, passed in the early twenties, restricted access to the Democratic primaries to white persons and excluded, by statute, black persons or Negroes from voting in those primaries. A black dentist from El Paso named Lawrence Nixon challenged that law and succeeded in having it thrown out by the Supreme Court in 1927. Over the ensuing years, the tug-of-war centered around efforts to achieve the same effect without having such a heavy color of state action. It ended in 1944 when the Supreme Court ruled with finality that those primaries were under state action and disallowed the state's effort to delegate its authorities in the areas of election and voting to private organizations which could then define their own membership and effectively exclude from the process people that they didn't like, in this instance black Texans.

The educational battlefront began here at the University with the efforts of Heman Sweatt in the late forties to attend the University's law school. That's an area in history some of you are familiar with. It's not a particularly pleasant era to recall. It's worth noting that in an attempt to keep Mr. Sweatt out of the UT Law School, he was offered classes in the basement of a building near the Capitol, where law professors were to come teach him law. Well, that didn't wash. Another effort was made with the establishment of an institution originally named the Texas State University for Negroes, now Texas Southern University in Houston. That institution in the opinion of the Supreme Court in late 1950 was deemed not to be separate and equal to the University of Texas; thus Heman Sweatt was allowed to enroll in law school. Thereafter Texas was primarily influenced by national developments: the *Brown* v. *Board of Education* decision, which had a profound impact, and subsequently the enactment of voting rights legislation.

The state's reaction to this sweeping change in this very sensitive area is interesting. It was certainly one of dedicated resistance, but primarily legal resistance. It perhaps is a distinctive factor with regard to Texas's treatment of this transitionary period that it was spared much of the violence and disruption that other parts of the South experienced. Perhaps this was because the forces of resistance resorted to the courts in order to try to maintain the status quo. This was particularly so with regard to the desegregation suits which came in the wake of the *Brown* decision. The state's response to the initiation of those suits is a revealing chapter.

The state decided to go after the NAACP and essentially attempted, as was done in other states, to shut the NAACP down. This was done by direct action of the Attorney General, who sent investigators out to raid NAACP offices around the state and gather evidence for use in a proceeding in Tyler, which sought to obtain an injunction to keep the organization from filing desegregation suits.

This was, on its surface, the enforcement of certain state statutes against barratry, which is defined as bringing frivolous lawsuits for profit. The NAACP was accused of that, and of not qualifying as a foreign corporation, the premise there being that the local branches of the NAACP were but mere extensions of a foreign corporation, the NAACP of New York. And pursuant to that effort, the organization was essentially harassed. Their plaintiffs in the lawsuits they had filed were picked up by investigators and by Texas Rangers and hauled into courts of inquiry and questioned as to their relationships with the attorneys, all in an effort to gain evidence for the barratry injunction, which did ensue.

Happily, a change in the administration, the attorney general's office, brought about a much more moderate climate, and that matter was eventually settled. The end result was that the NAACP was not permanently shut down in Texas.

The more recent advances, of course, were stimulated by the Civil Rights Act of 1964 and the subsequent Voting Rights Acts, both of which have had the effect of opening up many more of the benefits of citizenship to black and Hispanic Texans. I think that Congressman Pickle's comment earlier that the state has come a long way is appropriate. It mustn't lose sight of the fact that in this area we may have as far to go as we have come. There are residual elements of official resistance to full participation, as evidenced by the recent *Dallas Morning News* study regarding discrimination in the selection or exclusion of black citizens from jury trials in Dallas County, or indeed the nagging persistence of official segregation in certain housing units in East Texas.

However, Texans seem to have adopted a much more contemporary attitude toward these problems. They've evidenced a remarkable capacity to transform in this area and to embrace the ideals which they profess. The efforts of all citizens, of whatever hue, to achieve full participation in the society will continue. The spirit of black Texans—and the people I've referred to as black Texans do think of themselves as Texans—is best embodied by the lines from a poem entitled "And I Still Rise," by Maya Angelou.

> Out of the huts of history's shame,
> I rise
> Up from a past that's rooted in pain,
> I rise
> I am a black ocean, leaping and wide,
> Welling and swelling, I bear in the tide,
> Leaving behind nights of terror and fear,
> I rise.
> Into a daybreak that's wonderfully clear,
> I rise.

Bringing the gifts that my ancestors gave,
I am the dream and the hope of the slave.
I rise.
I rise.
I rise.

Diana Hobby: We are here to celebrate and to think about a state known to the world, as Alison Cook has pointed out, by the things that men do outdoors. From the Indian wars in the early days, to working cattle, to wrestling oil rigs, to football, there is a myth of the supporting women who fostered these male enterprises, diminished nowadays to the exhibition of furs and bangles in the sky boxes, and pompoms and pointy bras at half time on the field. I distrust that myth profoundly.

The Texas historian Celia Eckhardt has recently conducted a poll among Texas women, and none of them identifies her own experience with these legends. Responding to the poll's questions, Betty Dooley, director of the congressional caucus for women's issues in Washington, said, "I've come to believe that the morons, thieves and cutthroats who, with their women, settled Texas have passed on genetically a spirit of independence, courage and tenacity which has given me an edge over those defeated, pessimistic and cynical easterners."

So what books did we Texas mothers give our children to read about their heritage? The best then I think were John Graves's *Goodbye to a River* and Larry McMurtry's *In a Narrow Grave*. These were exercises in self-understanding, wonderful and powerful, but these men's self-understanding saw no need to listen to the opposite sex. In a combined bibliography of fifty titles, only three are by women. As every mother knows, our children went on from these approved texts to the selected works of Dan Jenkins and Larry King. Celia Eckhardt has transposed to Larry King what John Jay Chapman said about Emerson, that the worst Italian opera can teach a visitor from Mars what the collected works of Emerson cannot: that there are two sexes.

Larry King footnotes himself on the subject of women. In a reference to Chick Starter, he identifies it for his readers:

"Not a new aphrodisiac for hippie girls, but a product to feed infant chickens." For even the best of our male fiction writers writing about Texas show women on the periphery, or they imagine lives you'd hate to share. One of James Michener's female characters, a professor at TCU, says, "If I were—and God should be so generous—nineteen, with an eighteen-inch waist, flawless skin and flashing green eyes, I'd rather live in Texas than anywhere else. But if I were the way I actually was at that age, a thirty-one-inch waist, a soggy complexion and an IQ hovering near a hundred and sixty, Texas would not be my chosen residence."

Larry McMurtry has described early Texas as masculine and appealing because it offers an acceptable orientation to violence, leaving the exploration of complex modern life and women for the simplicities of the old ethos. Writing about the frontier in fiction, the Texas-educated critic John Irwin described the frontier scene in American life as the "spatial solution to temporal problems." The Texas frontier saluted the inexhaustible access to the original world, a generational metaphor for the unlimited now seen as closed to us by our parents, which is a very Freudian view. So does Faulkner's world of violent men reflect this diminished access to the world of masculine myth. "The Spotted Ponies" episode in *The Hamlet* is typical, in which the men squander their wives' meager family holdings to buy male wildness, the useless horses, which symbolize power, defying the conservator figures, the women who are scraping to keep their families.

Larry McMurtry's wonderful figure Clara should have written Texas history, but Larry has done for her the next best thing. She tells the widely acclaimed hero of *Lonesome Dove,* Woodrow Call, "You're a vain coward for all your fighting. I despised you then and I despise you now. You think you've always done right. That's your ugly pride, Mr. Call, but you never did right, and it would be a sad woman who ever needed anything from you."

The kinds of things that women like Clara did in Texas were no more mundane than following cows' rumps hundreds of miles to Kansas City. Yet the cowboy has been made into a figure of romance, and women like her have not. They have come to be known and written of, however, through exhibitions like "Women in Texas," which Anne Richards originated and organized, and Robert Caro's powerful description of what poverty meant in his book on the Texas of our President Johnson's youth. In the chapter called "The Sad Irons," he describes the hewing of wood and the drawing of water which was done the day before the day the real work of washing and ironing began.

Fifteen years ago the field of women's history didn't exist. Today well over a thousand U.S. scholars work in women's history, according to Mary Beth Norton, professor at Cornell. What has made the difference? Historians, like other people, want to study topics that seem relevant to their own experience. Thus it was when the children of immigrants became historians that the history of immigration began to attract attention. Women's historians now question not only the content of knowledge about women, but the categories used to organize that knowledge. For example, male economists looked at work as wage labor. The bulk of women's work was never wage labor. Society ran on it but it happened at home, and we know now that housework, too, has a history. That history is now politics: the traditional concerns of women, on the outside of wars and cattle drives, of football and hoked-up commercialism. Then as now, those concerns were public education, health, the care of the young and of the old, where we have been and whither we go, all the skills of mental and practical life as it must be lived now, when the frontier is closed, when Eden lies behind us and not ahead, when the masculine myth of heroic violence is a tale long told around hearths still to be tended, homes to be shored up against ruin, children to be taught the frontiers of the imagination, as Larry has told us, of love and the use of the art and the craft of life.

Joe B. Frantz: Whether your residence is Wizard Wells or Waco or Wichita Falls, you have another love always, which is San Antonio. It's kind of like that other woman or other man that you remember from your high school days, that you never quite surrender. And no one surrenders San Antonio, which is one of the memorable cities in the United States.

Now, twenty-five years ago, San Antonio tried to elect and did elect a Mexican-American, Henry Gonzalez, to Congress. The outcry from the status quo people in Texas was frantic: "This is the end of Texas. This is the end of San Antonio. This is the end of everything." Henry Gonzalez has been up there now for a quarter of a century and basically is an establishment figure because he's a way of life, a fact of life. And San Antonio has proved it was not the end of the world, and furthermore they have given us an Aggie of whom I approve, Henry Cisneros.

Henry Cisneros: Professor Frantz, thank you for your very apt paraphrasing of Sidney Lanier's comment of the 1890s, when he said that every Texan has two homes: one is where he or she lives today, and the other is San Antonio. I appreciate your reference to our city in that way.

You also referred to the Texas of before 1836 in your opening remarks, and I appreciate that, but I think we must also acknowledge the Texas of pre-1691, before that expedition of Governor Domingo Teran de los Rios, who first arrived on the banks of what is now the San Antonio River, arrived there on the feast day of St. Anthony, and so he named it for that saint, San Antonio, in March of 1691. There was a Texas even before 1527, when Cabeza de Vaca began in what is now Galveston and walked across Texas in that seven-year period that ended in Baja California. I refer to the Texas of hundreds of years before that era, a Texas which was populated and had human settlements. The place where I live today had a name for hundreds of years before the Spaniards ever arrived there; the Indians of the tribe known as the Payaya called it Yanaguana, and the word in the dialect of the Payaya meant "The Place of the Restful Waters." It was that same San Antonio River that we enjoy today that the Payaya referred to then. Where we sit now, here on the edges of the Texas Hill Country and the hills to the west of here, and then the plains beyond, was the Apacheria and the Comancheria. We have to at least acknowledge the existence of a Texas long before the Europeans ever arrived. It was the Texas of the Indians who roamed and tried to tame these regions.

My task today is to talk a little bit about one dimension of the change that's sweeping our state. There are many winds of change, of course, demographic and economic, but one dimension of change is the transformation of Texas into an urban state. The fact is that the people of Texas, the power of Texas, the focus on the problems of our state are occurring in the cities of Texas. We adhere to the myth of the open spaces, the Texas of cowboys and the range and the herds. Those dominate our myths of Texas, but the truth is that there isn't a more urban state in America. There isn't another state in America that the census defines as having twenty-eight metropolitan areas within its boundaries. By the time the mid-1990s roll around, a state of some fifteen million people today will have over twenty million people—phenomenal growth when you stop and try to analyze what that means. This is the year of the sesquicentennial, and it took us a hundred and fifty years to achieve a population of fifteen million. Over the course of the next ten or twelve or fifteen years at the most, we will have one-third again that number. I suspect that 90 per cent of those will be living in urban areas, in the cities of Texas. So the numbers will become even more graphic.

Not since 1865 has one state in America had three cities within it that were ranked among the top ten most populous in the country. The last time that happened it was the state of New York. New York then had New York City and Buffalo and the independent city of Brooklyn that were ranked among the top ten most populous cities in America. It didn't happen again in the westward expansion through Ohio or Illinois or even in California in the fifties and sixties. The next time it will occur is in the 1990 census. It's a fact now, but it will be documented in the 1990 census, when

Houston and Dallas and San Antonio are all three ranked among the top ten most populous.

If you look at the fastest-growing small communities in the country, in the seventies, the fifteen fastest-growing small SMSAs, seven of those fifteen, almost half in the entire country, were in Texas. They include places like College Station, Longview, Midland-Odessa, Edinburg, Harlingen, and McAllen. So it's no question that this will be a continuing and even more important phenomenon in our state. It will dominate our politics, dominate our thinking about how we confront the problems of Texas. The critical public issues will no longer be the problems of the range. They will be problems of how we build highways and schools and educate our people and live together in the cities of our state.

The cities and the towns, the urban areas of Texas, have been important throughout our entire history, from the Indian era when there were human settlements like Yanaguana, or when the Spanish grouped in the missions that they built in Los Adaes, near what is now Nacogdoches, to evangelize among the Indians and defend that part of Texas from the French incursion in Louisiana. El Paso del Norte and San Antonio were both contributions of the Spaniards to the urban places of Texas. In the period of independence we saw a growth of communities, big ones like Dallas and Houston and small places like Littlefield and Weatherford that grew out of the ranching experience, out of the building of Texas institutions that followed independence. The oil and gas boom brought us places like Kilgore and the massive development of the Houston oil technology base. The development of Athens on the plains brought us places like Wichita Falls, for example, and Midland and Dallas, where people from the ranch country came to invest and to bank and to buy and to build some semblance of culture in rural Texas.

Throughout that period, Texas was dominated by its basic industries and its towns. Its urban areas took the shape that oil and gas and agribusiness gave it. Today we are living in a period of immense change, and I suspect that the towns and cities of Texas after this period are going to take a decidedly different shape.

If we were to drive around the major communities of our state today and drive the perimeter of Texas, we would be shocked this morning at the human conditions we would find because of the problems of some of our basic industries. If our drive started in Beaumont and Port Arthur and Orange, we would be shocked to find 20 per cent unemployment, refinery closures still going on, and all of the human urban problems associated with the decline of those communities.

A drive then from there over to Houston would reflect high vacancy rates in office buildings and high rates of foreclosure in businesses, real estate problems associated with that community's heavy reliance on oil and gas, building an entire urban system around one basic industry, oil and gas and petrochemicals.

If our drive then took us down along the Gulf and we reached Brownsville and Harlingen and McAllen, drove up along the border past Laredo to Eagle Pass and Del Rio and out to El Paso, what we would find there would shock us also. It's the same basic problem: reliance on one major industry. But there it's not oil and gas, it's Mexico. And as the Mexican peso fell from twenty-five pesos to the dollar in 1982 to five hundred pesos to the dollar, roughly, at this time, in those communities unemployment rates rose to 30 per cent, and horrible problems, real human suffering, hunger in places like Rio Grande City in Starr County. If we were today to walk through the downtown streets of Eagle Pass, we would see one boarded-up store after another: a community that relied totally on the Mexican economy. It is paying the price for that lack of diversity today.

If our drive then took us up from the border and up past Midland-Odessa, we would see a community battered by oil and gas declines. Then up into the High Plains, up into Lubbock and Amarillo, we would see communities not nearly as badly hit, but nevertheless because of their dependence on one major industry, in that case agribusiness, stagnant commodity prices have taken their toll in that part of the state.

If our drive then took us across the top of the state and over into East Texas, we'd find some bright spots. There's a lot of wealth in places like Longview and Tyler, but there's also a lot of poverty. And places like Kilgore in East Texas are hurt dramatically by their dependence on oil and gas.

If I've painted a picture of some difficulty around the perimeter of Texas, the picture down the center of the core of the state is troublesome but not as troubled. In the Metroplex, Dallas-Fort Worth, Sherman-Denison, and the communities that surround the Dallas-Fort Worth area down into Waco and Temple and Belton and into Austin and down into San Antonio, we find unemployment rates that are higher than we'd like. They are 6 per cent where we had 4 per cent a couple of years ago. But they're not the 20s. They're not the 25s, and they're not the 30 per cents that confront some of the other parts of our state.

There's a lesson, I think, in the difference. The lesson is that some parts of Texas allowed themselves to be hitched totally to the economy and the culture of the Texas of the past, and some parts of the state are attempting and have been working hard to diversify their base, and to rely on the next economy of Texas and the next economy of the United States.

There's no question but that Texas in the year 2000 is going to be a more urban state. It will be the second most populous state in America, some distance behind California but having passed New York. With that will come all of the responsibilities and burdens of managing a heavy industrial, urban state. Texas in the year 2000 has a kind of science-fiction ring to it, but the year 2000 is only fourteen years from now. If you can remember what you were doing in 1972, then that's the distance from this moment to the year 2000. It's just not that far. Those of you who are forty years old will be fifty-four and not in a much different state of life than what you are right this moment in the year 2000.

The decisions that will shape Texas in the year 2000 are being made right now. If we're not thinking about them now, if we're not planning them now, the chances are in the year 2000 they will not have been achieved.

So what will the urban areas of Texas be like in the year 2000, realistically? I suspect the Dallas-Fort Worth area is going to be one of the strongest geographic areas in the country because it is so diverse. That's not a completely untroubled picture, because the Dallas-Fort Worth area will take on some of the feel of the Los Angeles Basin: sprawled, multiple communities, overlapping jurisdictions, very difficult to create regional solutions because of the vast diversity and the jurisdictional problems that will confront that area. It will be conservative and it will be positive in its orientation, and in that sense perhaps a little different than the Los Angeles Basin. But some of the fundamental urban problems that confront that basin of fourteen million people today will characterize Dallas-Fort Worth with some five million people or so in the year 2000.

Houston will work hard in the years between now and then to diversify its economy, but I suspect that it will still be troubled by its reliance on oil and gas, and its rate of growth will not be as strong between now and the year 2000.

The Valley, unfortunately, will continue to be poor. Problems in Mexico and Central America, which will take years to resolve, will result in a continuing emigration. As fast as efforts are made to increase the economy of the Valley, poor people coming in and filling the barrel from the bottom will keep poverty statistics high, incomes low, and human problems severe. The Valley will be a problem in that sense for the rest of the state.

West Texas will have begun to wrestle with but probably not have resolved its problems of water and agriculture. As a result, I don't expect a whole lot of growth in Lubbock and Amarillo, though I think they'll probably be able to hold their own. A lot of the solution for that area of the state is going to depend on how the state resolves issues of funding of Texas Tech, for example, and whether or not that institution can create new economic opportunities for that area.

Beaumont-Port Arthur I suspect will continue to be plagued by the problems it has today because of the fundamentally structural problems that confront that part of our state.

So Texas will have changed by the year 2000. Demographics will be different. Billy Reagan tells me that in the Houston School District today the majority of children under the fifth grade, the majority of children in the Houston system, which covers that entire city, are either Hispanic or black or Asian. I suspect as that population group moves through, it will shape the look of Houston demographically. It will be important culturally in Texas that we begin to think in terms of inclusiveness, not the exclusive approaches to how we make decisions or inform people, but how we bring people together. That demographic change is not something to be afraid of, as long as we're patient and as long as we involve the dialogue that allows people to make decisions together about their destinies.

I suspect that Texas in the urban areas between now and the year 2000 will work hard to diversify, but that's a tough call. It will mean unprecedented emphasis on education and new approaches to financing. It will mean relating to the global economy as we've never done before.

Perhaps most important, though, as we confront the cultural issues that will shape urban Texas between now and the year 2000, is a cultural concession. Although we like to think of ourselves as rugged individuals, every one of us able to stand on a plateau out in the Fort Davis Mountains and be masters of our destiny over everything we see within our reach, the truth of the matter is that we must live in crowded urban places and concede something of our rights in relationships with other people.

I have that experience myself frequently, of visiting a ranch and of thinking how wonderful it would be to control everything in sight, from horses and cattle to the rough land, and then going back, as mayor of my city, to a poor parish and being humbled by citizens who demand the basics that we've not been able to produce for them, and knowing that it's impossible any longer to think in terms of that absolute rugged individualism, but instead the interlocked web of destinies that I think is the lot of Texans.

We must decide to decide on some of the important questions. Muddling through, leaving them for time to bring out, hoping that a Ross Perot will step to the front or another Jesse Jones will solve them, is not going to be enough. We've got to decide to decide some of these questions, to set some targets and goals and decide that we want to work together, based on cooperation and a measure of consensus.

Texas is at a juncture, and faces some difficult choices. And so I close my remarks with a favorite poem which speaks to that sense of choice at a juncture. It's a poem many of you know by Robert Frost called "The Road Not Taken." It talks of the symbols of his native New England and New Hampshire, which is rough and difficult and rocky, and reminds me, when I read his work, frequently of Texas, a place where the land has shaped the people. In this poem he talks about a man who comes to a crossing of the roads, a fork in the road, as he approaches a wood. And one is a road that seems to have been traveled before. There are leaves down and they're blackened as human feet have trod them. It's a somewhat softer and easier path. Down the other road is a somewhat more treacherous way, which clearly hasn't been traveled nearly as frequently. He closes his poem by saying:

> Two roads diverged in a wood,
> And I took the one less traveled by,
> And that has made all the difference.

I don't think there are many states in our country or many places of government in America which have traveled down the road that I think Texas must. It's a road of consensus-building, of bringing people together, of pragmatism and finding new approaches that are neither liberal nor conservative, or Democratic or Republican, but just things that work and that are entrepreneurial. Some states have. I think North Carolina probably has, and one could make the case that in building its great educational system after the war California did. Massachusetts in recent years has made some of those kinds of concessions to the collective body of the people of Massachusetts. I suspect those are some of the challenges that are before Texas. It is the road less traveled by, but it's also the road that will make all the difference.

Joe B. Frantz: I liked your ranch reference, because that to me is one of the biggest myths we've been sold in this state. We used to like to think and still think to a great extent that we did it all with no help from anybody. It was all there. It was a myth at the time, a saying at the time, a cliche that later got Texanized, that all of this belongs to God, Sears-Roebuck, and the federal government. And we did not do it ourselves. I stood out there in the 1880s or whenever, on those wide-open acres and looked about me, and tended my cattle, and yes, I did my work myself, or directed people to do it, but the Republic of Texas or the State of Texas, or the federal government in other states, if you want to get outside the state, provided the land and the water and mineral wealth. I paid nothing for it, except just to be there and to fight nature.

Which is not to diminish what they did. But the West, including Texas, has been the most heavily subsidized section of the United States since its beginning. We have lived off the government's largess, and of course that's running out now. And we no longer follow the same industries, for very obvious reasons.

But we won a lottery ticket, in effect, and for generations we hardly had to think. In Texas, when the range cattle industry ran out, in came Spindletop, and we're just now getting to the point where we have to think. It reminds me very much of a youngster who has a big inheritance and grows up to be attractive, a little troublesome, immature. And about the time his inheritance runs out, he gets a second one. So he remains attractive and troublesome and immature. Then one day he's got to go to work and he's got to think. We have reached that mature stage now where we are going to have to think more than we have had to in the past.

Henry Cisneros: I'd like to add a couple of thoughts, if I could. First is this. It's really sort of a simple point, but it was made by *Texas Business* magazine in a piece that they did about a year ago. It talked about the difference between Texas and California. Texas has been able to build off the bounty of the earth. We were fortunate that Mother Nature put oil under the ground and made the topography and the climate hospitable to cattle and sorghum and cotton. Granted, it took smart people and courageous people and tough people, but if it hadn't been there because of the bounty of the earth, all of that would have been for naught. We're lucky.

California, on the other hand, in the last forty years or so anyway, has relied on the bounty of its people, building a great university system, and as a result has prepared itself for the next economy. If it were a nation, California, it would be the sixth most powerful nation in the world economically. The greatest aggregation of technological know-how in the world in one physical place is Silicon Valley, and the aerospace industry south of Los Angeles, and the emerging technology in San Diego, et cetera. While we're in a slump, there they have had minor cyclical kinds of things but they're strong.

Point one is that point about investing in the bounty of our people. But I don't think we're prepared to invest in our people yet. We haven't really crossed over the threshold of some very critical decisions about whether or not we really value all our people in Texas.

I was in California about a month ago, invited to come out to Cal Tech University, where Cal Tech sponsored a study on the future of California ethnically, the demographic changes occurring in California that are going to shake that state to its foundations. And they're trying to get ready. In 1940, if I remember the numbers correctly, California was a state of 80 per cent white. In the year 2005, maybe 2010, this study suggested California will have no dominant majority. California will be 25 per cent Asian, 25 per cent black, 25 per cent Hispanic, and 25 per cent white. Fundamental political, institutional, educational challenges before it, but they're getting ready.

Now, compare that with our institutions in Texas. I serve on the board of regents of Texas A&M, and I asked the other day for the data on our minority enrollment at Texas A&M. Hispanics, who are about 17 per cent of the state, are 4 per cent of the student body at Texas A&M, and blacks, who are about 15 per cent of the state, are about 3 per cent of the student body at Texas A&M, for a total of about 7 per cent of the student body who are minority. And there are no dramatically powerful or effective efforts to change that.

I chose the institution that I am associated with in the spirit of self-criticism, but I think very nearly the same criticism could be made of the University of Texas. There's not really much intent there, much seriousness about it. Certainly not sufficiently serious when one acknowledges what the shape of Texas will be fifteen or twenty years from now. Failure to educate—this is not something we ought to do for somebody else, for people who are brown or black, but it's something we ought to do for Texas, because those people are going to be producing legislators who are mad, angry; they're going to be producing people who feel cheated because the system never worked for them.

I think we've got tough days ahead unless we confront some of those kinds of questions. I think California has done a better job on that score than we have. You get a real sense of the mix out there and you don't get it here in Texas. That's not a criticism; it's just a statement of one of the major challenges that I don't think we've come to terms with yet. Now it's coming.

I was out in Littlefield, Texas, just north of Lubbock, the other day. In Littlefield just a little bit less than half of the population is Hispanic, and they're trying to work together. But I suspect that if we were to go to Tyler today, the difference between what the oil families think of as solutions and what the black community thinks of as solutions are miles and miles apart. I think we've got a long way to go yet on that point and we're not working on it as hard as we ought to be.

Norman Bonner: The politics of inclusion is what you captioned all of that under. Alison referred to the increasing numbers of Asian students who are coming out at the tops of their graduating classes. Clearly the challenge to the state is to find a way to draw upon all the resources of all its people, as opposed to continuing to practice the politics of exclusion, which is based on the very faulty and dangerous premise that only a very narrow segment of the population has a corner on all the wisdom necessary to build wealth, run the state, and face the future.

I agree wholeheartedly with the Mayor that it is critical for the state to embrace all segments of the population, recognize that every segment of the population has individuals with remarkable skills and talents that all of the state needs. The politics of exclusion, of privilege, of excluding minority groups or women, is certainly a relic of the past and should be laid to rest with the dinosaur.

Alison Cook: There are times when I think that the only cultural artifact that all of Texas's very differentiated groups, Anglo, Hispanic, black, even Asian, really understand, really agree on, and I say this in total seriousness, is the jalapeño. How do we go about deciding to decide what we want from each other, and why have we not done it?

Henry Cisneros: Those things don't happen by accident, people coming together and finding out where they want to go. They don't happen by accident. They don't happen in genteel social settings and occasional social contacts. There have to be some structures whereby you get folks together and get them to really brainstorm and think hard and imaginatively and leave their cynicism at the door, leave the normal blinders, the limits on imagination at the door, and just come into forums and talk about what can be. We tried that in San Antonio; we had a process we called Target 90. It involved about five hundred folks. We just asked, "What do we want San Antonio to be in 1990?" Knowing that if we weren't thinking about it in 1983, three years ago, it wasn't going to happen.

Now, that process has not been perfect, to be sure. But enough places like it that Corpus Christi set something called CC 90, Dallas has efforts underway, and I think Austin has experimented with it. Lots of communities across the state are realizing that this cultural transition from waiting for time to bring us out okay, to somehow becoming masters of our own destinies, is a major step. It's a psychological step that has to be made, and it's not going to happen by accident. It's only going to happen when you bring people together with the purpose of trying to ask some of those questions.

It's a naive notion, perhaps; I thought so at the beginning in San Antonio. It worked for us. Maybe it doesn't work for a whole state; I think it works for regions probably. But I know that sitting around reading about it and hoping for it and criticizing each other is not going to bring us out. I know that for a fact.

Larry McMurtry: Texas is finally arriving at a recognition of the sort that I've labored with all my life. We are one of the most optimistic states in an optimistic nation, and optimistic for quite a number of good reasons, because we have had a very progressive society virtually for our entire history.

The novelist, or the writer, or the artist, is a little different in his assumptions, or her assumptions, from many members of the society. In an optimistic society you grow up with the belief that you go to school, you educate yourself, you learn a craft, you learn a trade. Then you go out in life, and you practice it. If you exert yourself and acquire discipline and don't let up, you can get better and better and better at it for your entire life. And it's a consistent upward graph.

Many people in my little hometown, which is now devastated by the oil bust, have lived with this assumption their entire lives and have seen no reason to doubt it, because things have gotten better and better and better out there, up until about six months ago. But the artist knows that he doesn't work in a progressive trade. It's nice that I won the Pulitzer Prize yesterday; it doesn't mean that when I sit down to write tomorrow I will be able to write a better book than *Lonesome Dove* or *Terms of Endearment*. The arts are not progressive. It's actually more natural that at some point in your career, instead of getting better, you start getting worse. This has happened to almost all writers who have ever lived. A very few, very great writers are spared by a kind of recovery, which can come very late, and this occasionally occurs with poets, like Mr. Yeats or William Carlos Williams. In order to achieve it, unfortunately, they had to go crazy and break down the psychic defenses that kept them from getting deeper into their work.

I'm not saying that Texas has to go crazy—some people already think it's crazy—in order to deepen and enrich itself. But it does have to come to grips with the basic psychological fact that societies are not necessarily and inevitably progressive either. In order to progress, at some point they have to acquire new skills. They have to plumb their resources more deeply and more consciously than perhaps they have. There have been so many givens in this state. There is so much here that essentially only had to be used and exploited, didn't have to be planned particularly. As the Mayor just said, we've now reached the state where we aren't naturally and inevitably going to progress. We'll progress only if we think hard enough and plan.

Joe B. Frantz: In the way of summation, what we've done is raise the questions. We are worried, obviously, about Texas of the future. We are not content to live on our past. Mr. Bonner said we did a halfway dignified job of bringing our minorities up to a fairly equal status with some residues still to be cleaned out. As was also suggested, we are kind of Dickensian, Mr. Micawber, I guess, in the fact we think something will turn up; it always has. But we're facing the fact that right now it is not in sight. We're making insufficient efforts to find out what that something that's going to turn up is and then go out and solicit it and invite it in.

I don't want to get overpolitical, but I'm getting elderly enough now that I don't have any self-interest. I feel that one of the most dangerous things going around this state, which is national, eternal, is this "no new taxes" shibboleth we're hung on. Taxes, properly used, are an investment. We need to invest in the minds of Texans, particularly young Texans, to make sure that we turn out our only discernible resources of the future, now. Those resources are all the people somewhere just born, up to the age where they're still willing to take in some education; let's get them trained, make them useful, give them dimension, give them enough background that they can have insights. When we are willing to let them have less than the best because we don't want any new taxes, as a slogan, we are cheating our children and our grandchildren.

We've all run into James Michener around here in the past several years. He represents to an astonishing degree—it won't work for most of us—what can happen. An orphan boy, a poor boy, no prospects but bright, he was given scholarships to go to college. He figured that altogether someone, some entity invested about eight-five hundred dollars in getting him through college. He has generated at his latest figure about eighty million dollars worth of income through his books, his movies—not all to him, but through the things that have been done because of what came out of his mind and the opportunity. That is a rate of return that we'd all like to experience. I would invest in that; I would pay something, part of that eighty-five hundred, if I could have it back in proportion. That's one place that I think we are remiss if we do not see the opportunity.

POLITICS AND ECONOMY

George Christian: Our distinguished panel has the responsibility to relate the economic growth of Texas, from the centennial of 1936 until the sesquicentennial of 1986, to our particular brand of politics. We'll explore several questions: How much influence has business had in politics? Is it a positive influence or is there something sinister about it? What's the impact of our conversion from one-party politics to political parity in Texas? What's been the quality of our leadership in government and in business? We'll look at the Texas Legislature, which is the strongest arm of our state government, and talk about how it's changed. We'll talk about the politics of oil and gas, which has been our most consistently powerful industry during this fifty-year period. Our task is to decide where we've been and where we are. We're going to leave it up to the afternoon panel to tell us where we're going. The panelists include two outstanding political writers, two outstanding lawyer-legislators, a scholar who is an expert on oil and gas, and a businessman whose long career encompasses two of our major industries, utilities and construction.

My concept of change in Texas is that it's rarely been swift, not very dramatic, mostly deliberate, and often reluctant. It's more like a Gulf breeze than a West Texas blue norther. No one could doubt, however, that we've come a long way since the centennial of 1936, which some in this room remember. In those days of the mid-thirties, the farmers were in trouble. The banks were struggling. The government was trying to save the oil industry. There were wars in Africa and the Mediterranean. All of Europe was very nervous, and the Bolsheviks were threatening all we hold dear. We indeed have come a long way.

While in some ways we may be back where we started, let's consider some of the other aspects of change. This fifty years has been the age of the dam builders, the highway constructors, the oil-well drillers. All of them have changed the face of this state. During this span of time we've moved into plastics and chemicals. We've air-conditioned our cities and made them magnets for great growth. Our people have been restless, moving into the towns to find work, especially during World War II. They have, by their migrations, forever altered the rural flavor of our history. Yet anyone who knows anything about Texas politics knows that the small-town ethic prevails in that arena, notwithstanding population shifts and one man-one vote.

Jim Crow has died hard in this state, yet the racial barriers have come down in most respects. Our children today can barely conceive of the way it was in this state just a few years ago. Today we have major differences among ourselves in this state, but all of those differences together, collectively, can't compare to the malignancy of racial segregation.

Our politics has been basically conservative with a few odd liberals thrown in here and there. Change has come through a conservative establishment, sometimes reluctantly, and sometimes from a dazzling display of leadership, as in the years immediately following the war. Yet the politician who had the most profound effect on this state represented a duke's mixture of New Deal liberalism and rock-solid capitalism. Lyndon Johnson cast his shadow over Texas through most of this period in a way that no other political figure can match.

We've supplied the nation with some other stars as well as a few charlatans and bumpkins. Politically, we've never been as wild as our sister state of Louisiana, which is still the northernmost banana republic. But we have had our day in the sun. We've produced some characters who have made an imprint on this state. We've produced businessmen who have made a tremendous imprint on politics, and we've produced politicians who have made quite an imprint on the growth and progress of this state.

T. Louis Austin: It's going to be a short speech if I answer that question: how does business cope with legislation? We don't. But I've worked in politics in this state for a long time, and my basic thrust was to always try to talk to my enemies. I first started out with Charlie Wilson when he was a state senator from Lufkin. He was running with the Public Utility Commission bill that I didn't want and he wanted. The *Texas Observer* wrote an article about this, and they had a David-Goliath cartoon with Charlie being David, and Austin and the rest of the utilities being Goliath. It was a little cartoon, but Charlie blew it up into a big framed picture. It's still on my wall at home now. Above Goliath, he put "Bad Louie." Under David he put "Good Charlie." So to this good day if I want to get into Charlie Wilson's office, I don't say, "I'm Louis Austin." I say, "Bad Louie's here, let me see him." And I get a lot of results.

If everything goes according to what we are supposed to do, I understand another panelist here will talk about how the "fat cats" have run the state. I'm just beginning to understand why Max Sherman got me up here. He had all those intellects on that first panel, and he's got politicians and writers and brains on this panel. He had to have one nerd, so he got me. But being sort of an in-house polluter, raiser of rates, contractor, highway builder, nuclear power plant builder, "fat cat" of this state, I'll talk a little.

I think we've made a lot of mistakes, and I'm looking forward to this afternoon, because then we will see what it's going to be in the future. But we in business look at the politicians and we say, "The way to solve this problem is throw money at it. Hire another lobbyist, get another slick campaign, get somebody to work, get more money in the PAC, and throw money at it." The politicians of this state and the United States look at business and say, "Well, socialism has never played in Peoria, so we don't want to own all of this, so just regulate it to death." And they've just about done that. You know, our law schools are turning out lawyers, about ten for every one that we need. But you've got to have them because we're so regulated that every step I take, I'm exposing myself to either a million-dollar liability or a jail term. I ain't got many million dollars, and I ain't got many years left in my life for jail terms.

In my opinion, this is not the way to go. I think that we should try to build consensus, as Mayor Cisneros said of some of our social problems. If the business of the United States and the government of the United States do not start working together, we are going to be licked by the rest of the world. I've spent some time talking to my enemies. We did a lot of this in the coal policy project, where we got the president of the Sierra Club and the president of a number of coal companies to sit down in a room. This is not the place to do it. You see, I'm spouting off here trying to make a point. Every one of these is going to be spouting off here trying to make a point. You testify before some committee, and you're trying to get something over. We have so overdemocratized this country that we no longer have smoke-filled rooms. I don't think you can run a good democracy without a smoke-filled room. There you can state your position and get the other guy to state his position. You're this far apart, without having fifteen reporters and forty-five TV commentators at night to tell everybody what you said. I love the press, but that strains my love sometimes.

The big problem in the United States is still getting a consensus. I have worked with the Sierra Club. I have worked with the environmental defense fund. I have worked with the consumer groups, and I have found those to be real nice people. Before we start talking, we hate one another's guts. Yet if we sit down, it's just like Will Rogers, who said that he never met a guy he didn't like. Some people say he hadn't met some people, but that's all right. There is a lot of consensus-building out there that we can do to put this nation back on the right track.

We are still in an experiment in this nation: all of the problems that the other panel talked about. Nobody ever wrote a book before 1776 about how you run a democracy and how you have free business and how you have a free government. So we still have an experiment going here. In seeking perfection, I wish we wouldn't destroy the good. Many times we want perfection. I cannot give you a perfect society from business, because it's run with people. People make mistakes, and we can't give people perfect cars and perfect roads and perfect this. We can do a good job, but we don't do a perfect job.

So my plea to the politicians and the businessmen is to talk. You know, a politician will vote on anything if you get everybody on your side. I go in to see Bill Messer one day and someone else comes in to see him the next. But if you get us together and get a consensus, then we can make this a great nation.

I have a great hope for Texas, in spite of all of the apologies we make about the men doing everything outdoors and women behind it. In fact my wife has got a note pad that says, "Behind every successful man is a woman that made it necessary." And if you could see my bills at the end of every month, you'd know why I'm successful, if that's true. But we made it not only as Texans but as a nation and as a world because there was always somebody looking after us. And man started out eating the forbidden fruit, and then we slew our brothers, and then we shot the messengers in the form of the prophets that came with messages that we didn't want to hear, and we crucified a Christ, and we enslaved our other brothers, and we spawned a Hitler. But we made it from the Garden of Eden to the LBJ Library in Austin, Texas, because somebody was looking after us. And there is enough brain power in this state to solve every problem we've got: mass transit, poverty, politics, hatred, race, everything, but it must be honest people sitting down, seeking honest solutions, and not trying to find scapegoats.

George Christian: I want you to note that Louis listed politics along with other problems like poverty.

Cyndi Taylor Krier: I was challenged, when I was first invited to address this sesquicentennial forum, at the thought of summarizing one hundred and fifty years of political history in five minutes. They then told me, no, no, just focus on the last fifty years and the Republican Party, and I tried to make a trade where I could focus on the first one hundred years of the Republican Party in Texas and told them I could do that in five sentences. The Republican Party held power during Reconstruction from 1865 to 1874. Thereafter it failed to win another statewide election for almost a century. In 1914, the Republicans drew fewer votes than the Socialists in Texas. As late as 1942 the Republican gubernatorial candidate lost all two hundred and fifty-four counties. For the most part of the first half of the twentieth century, Republicans were more preoccupied with patronage when Republicans controlled the White House than we were with electing candidates to office in Texas. Fortunately for the Republican Party, though not for one who is trying to condense history, that began to change in the early fifties.

Most point to 1952, when Democratic Governor Allan Shivers and Democratic Senator Price Daniel endorsed Eisenhower for president, and when state Democrats cross-filed on both the Democratic and Republican ballots, as the beginning of our modern two-party state. Thus, as Larry McMurtry mentioned that he had lived through one-third of our Texas sesquicentennial years, virtually everybody in this room has lived through almost every significant historical occurrence within the Republican Party in Texas.

The Republican Party continued to grow over the past thirty years and captured its greatest victory since Reconstruction in the last election in 1984. Texas Republicans had won big in presidential elections before. In fact, in 1972 Nixon's landslide in Texas was greater than Reagan's was in 1984. Yet in 1972 there had been no substantial gains on congressional and legislative levels. In contrast, in 1984, while Republicans across the country largely were failing to capitalize on the Reagan victory, in Texas Republicans did. They retained control of the Tower Senate seat; they increased their numbers in Congress by four to an all-time record of ten; they reached record levels in the Texas Legislature, capturing more than a third of the House; they swept judicial races in Houston and Dallas and captured the sheriff's office in Tarrant County in Fort Worth and in my hometown of San Antonio. The victory was significant even in its defeat, because you saw token, unknown, unfinanced Republicans garner 45 per cent of the statewide vote against well-established Democrats in races for the Texas Supreme Court and the Railroad Commission.

Throughout this period, polls and surveys showed a marked growth in people who call themselves Republicans. Back in 1952, 66 per cent of Texans called themselves Democrats. A brave 6 per cent claimed to be Republicans. Even twenty years later in 1972 the split was still 57 to 14 per cent. But by the early eighties, just as many Texans were calling themselves Republicans as Democrats for the first time in Texas history. Rather than chronologically taking you through the last seventeen biennial elections, I've tried to extract what other political commentators and I have perceived as some trends during that time. You may not concur with all of them, you may dispute some of them, for I think analyzing what caused elections is just as imprecise a science as predicting them in advance.

I would attribute the growth of the two-party state in Texas over the past three-and-a-half decades to four key factors. The first, new Democrats. As liberals gained increasing prominence within the national and state Democratic Party, a conservative Republican Party in a conservative state benefitted, becoming the principal home for the Texas conservative majority. The second factor was new Republicans. Conservative Democrats who concluded there was no longer a place for them within the Democratic Party switched to the Republican Party. Despite a flurry in recent years, that's really not a new phenomenon and can be traced as far back as the fifties and through such noted Republicans as Tower, Clements, Connally, Gramm, Hance, and others who felt either ideologically more comfortable or politically more electable within the Republican Party.

The third factor would be new Texans, who tended to be predominantly Republican. In 1978 there was a poll conducted for the United States Senate race that showed six of ten eligible voters in that year had not voted in the 1972 election for the United States Senate, and that growth has continued on through the early eighties. Also, as Henry Cisneros discussed in more detail, there has been a shift within our state which also tended to work in favor of the Republican Party, as Texans moved from rural areas, which traditionally voted Democrat, into the urban areas where Republicans had greater strength.

Finally, we have the new voters. The Republican Party's newfound allegiance among younger voters could prove the most significant trend of all in the future, if it holds. The Texas poll in the eighties has cited among eighteen to twenty-nine-year-olds the Republican Party holding a 44 to 29 per cent lead over Democratic allegiance. Among older Texans, those over sixty-two years of age, Democrats still hold their traditional 49 to 23 per cent advantage.

Given the recent demographic trends, perhaps those political trends were almost inevitable. As our state became more suburban, more affluent, better educated, younger, with fewer native Texans, perhaps it is only natural that it would become less dependent on a one-party Democratic political process. So as we gather to discuss our sesquicentennial, one hundred and fifty years after our state's independence, I think we can conclude that the battle for Texas political independence, at least, has been won.

Bill Messer: I don't mind saying I'm not really going into full-time practice of law, I'm going into lobbying. As Molly said when I retired, I'm answering a lower calling. I didn't agree with that and don't agree with a lot of things Molly writes. But I read her every time because she is, I think, one of the most entertaining writers of the press.

The Texas Legislature today, in my estimation, is and basically always has been representative of Texans. The Texas Legislature is made up of the types of Texans that live in Victoria and Temple and McAllen and El Paso and Houston and Dallas. They bring with them a tradition.

The first Anglo Texans didn't come to set up a utopian society. They didn't come to seek religious freedom. They came for cheap farmland, and they were willing to give up their U.S. citizenship and become nominal Catholics to get it. The urbanization that's just been mentioned by George during the forties and fifties wasn't a move from the farm to the city to enjoy the metropolitan lifestyle. That was where you could make your fortune and that's where Texans went. The in-migration into Texas in the seventies from other states hasn't been the result of our fine climate down here. It's been because they perceived that there was economic opportunity in Texas and they wanted a piece of the pie. The same can be said of the illegal immigration of Mexican nationals into Texas in recent years. That is a voluntary, economically motivated migration.

So Texas is populated by citizens that believe that Texas offers economic opportunity. I don't think they're wrong, but I think that's why they came here. I think that's why they elect representatives to the Texas Legislature that are basically business-oriented pragmatists as opposed to social engineers or some other genre. The political tradition of the Texas Legislature is conservative and has been Democratic. Now, that's changing, as Cyndi has outlined for you. The maxim that "what's good for business is good for Texas" was accepted more often than it was debated for several decades. It's one that frankly I won't apologize for and subscribe to myself.

The one-party political system of the forties and fifties and sixties is changing because Texas is changing. But it was one that worked hand in hand with the business establishment, not necessarily big business, but one in which the small-town department store owner felt a commonality of interest with the richest oil man in Dallas or the biggest banker in Houston. It may not sound very noble, but even now we have a certain respect for the efficiency of a business-government oligarchy that's represented in Japan. Basically, that's what we had. It wasn't a big business-big government oligarchy. But for about three or four decades we had a conservative political establishment and a business establishment that worked together hand in glove. And it wasn't that bad. It wasn't a boss system, it was unobtrusive, it was basically scandal-free, and it did what Texans wanted done. That was to allow them to take their piece of the pie and to seek that economic opportunity they thought was there. It was done with a lot less ideological posturing than we see today. During this period, government tended to the business of business.

I think there are a couple of examples that exemplify that attitude of the Texas Legislature and its attitude that it was supposed to get involved and help business when it could. Fifty years ago, which is the frame of reference that we begin in, the Texas Legislature, with all its faith in the free enterprise system and its hallowed respect for personal property rights, decided that the best business decision would be to authorize the Railroad Commission to fix the price of oil. Thank goodness they did. They made the same business decision that OPEC made about thirty years later. And we have all reaped the benefits of it in our university system and our system of taxation in Texas and our economy. The other has already been mentioned. That is, although we were a conservative Democratic state, we didn't have that much trouble following Governor Shivers into the Republican Party to elect Ike Eisenhower if we made a good horse trade on the tidelands in the deal. That attitude exemplified what the legislature did during these years. It wasn't a legislature that sat back and let business go unnoticed and unaided. In fact, they felt that it was their job to help business every chance they could, and they did. They did the types of things that I think have benefitted most of us, like putting in the constitution a pay-as-you-go provision, right to work, things like that.

In the following decade, much of this has changed because of the demographic changes in Texas. In the seventies there were startling changes on the political scene that the Texas Legislatures dealt with. In 1972 we had our first single-member districts in Texas, and Republicans and minorities got their foothold in the legislature that they have held on to and nourished and have, in fact, grown. In 1975 the Voting Rights Act was applied to Texas. A massive voter registration of Hispanics and blacks that coincided resulted in drastic changes in politics in Texas and particularly the Democratic Party in Texas. In a two-year span you had the Democratic primary made up of 15 per cent black and brown go to 30 per cent black and brown. In conjunction with this was the in-migration of people from out of state who, whether Republicans or not, at least did not have a Democratic tradition and didn't understand the distinctions that native Texans made between the Texas Democratic Party and the national Democratic Party. They didn't understand that the affiliation of these Tory Democrats was with business as opposed to interest groups such as labor.

Today we've got a legislature that is still representative of the Texas population in spite of these changes. In the House we've got thirty-one minority members as compared to twelve in 1971. We've got fifty-two Republicans as compared to one in 1965. For all of the partisanship and factionalism that you might predict from these numbers or from the electoral returns that clearly indicate we are a two-party state, the legislature has not represented that kind of partisanship and factionalism. In fact, we're still doing business pretty much the way they did in years gone by. We still organize the House along ideological lines as opposed to party lines. We have a Republican, Ross Perot, who recommends to us that we equalize between richer and poorer school districts and pay teachers more and raise taxes to do it. We go right along with that because it's good for business, for one thing. Democrats raised tuition and cut state spending. Why? Because that's what the Texas population wants them to do. For all its diversity, for all of the Asians and Hispanics and blacks and Republicans and women, Texas is still a very homogeneous state. The people still have the same expectations of government and they agree on 95 per cent of what the state ought to be doing. They agree on what the issues are and they're willing to build consensus. They're willing to compromise and pragmatically address the problems. For that reason, the legislature agrees on what the issues are: public education, and highways, and health care for those who can't afford to pay for it, water development and water quality, and economic development. I'll note again that all this is good for business.

So we see the Texas Legislature doing things like reforming public education. In spite of the fact that money's really tight, tighter than it's been in recent memory, we're being pretty generous with universities. We enact two new social programs, indigent health care and a program to feed the hungry in Texas. We build highways, a massive new highway program paid for with user fees. We propose a water plan, which, by the way, is the most far-reaching environmental document that the Texas Legislature has ever passed. We pass a hazardous waste bill. As a recognition of the minority influence in the legislature, we cover farm workers with worker's comp and with unemployment comp. But before you lay all of that on the increased numbers of minority representatives, look how many Republicans voted for those same things and how many of us old dinosaurs did, too.

Of even more interest to me is how did we go about it? How did the legislature comport itself? Well, they did it the way the people wanted them to do it. They do it in a very open fashion, much more open than we used to. I will have to admit that I agree with Louis to some degree; you can't really run a very good legislature without some smoke-filled rooms. But we do it in an open fashion, and we do it in a business-like demeanor. The Texas Legislature isn't as colorful as it used to be. Molly has to look a little further back into history to find the good stories of the bumpkins. There are still a few that Molly can ferret out. But for the most part the House addresses these issues and is more likely to address these issues in the cool deliberation of a committee hearing as opposed to the heat of a floor debate. You're still going to see, in the House and the Senate, team votes. We talk about them a lot, but they're different team votes than they used to be. They are not orders that come down from on high and are expected to be followed unthinkingly. Team votes today involve school reform or a water package, and it's done after deliberation with a cross section of the House that is the leadership. During the last session of the legislature before each team vote, every member of the Texas House was called into the Speaker's office in groups of twenty and allowed to have his input and to change the course of the team.

Power has been decentralized. The average legislator today is under the scrutiny of the media and single-interest groups and a variety of lobbies. The number of registered lobbies has tripled in the last three legislative sessions. The Texas Legislature has responded to this scrutiny, in the staff that they have available and in the rules they operate under, so that we have an open process. We have rules that now allow for every standing committee to participate in the appropriative process in the House and that's had its effect. Basically, we have met the challenges of shifts in federalism, the changing political scenery of the state of Texas and the changing demographics. In contrast to Congress, we are still changing and we are still in transition, just as Texas is in transition. You look at Congress and you see the multiplicity of caucuses and study groups and committees and subcommittees and different interest groups. It is very hard to fix responsibility for the legislative process and, ultimately, for public policy making. But in Texas we have not committed the one unpardonable legislative sin of institutional gridlock. The Texas Legislature is still a vital, organic, changing, maturing, representative legislature, representative of the people of Texas. Today the people of Texas perceive that they are in transition as a state. They perceive that they are leaving the gilded age of oil and are moving into a progressive but still prosperous age that requires government to take more of a hand in managing that transition and doing it in an orderly fashion. That is good for business, too.

George Christian: I'll agree with Bill Messer that legislators today are a lot less colorful than they used to be. I remember one old-timer who used to never refer to a fact when he was speaking to the House of Representatives. He always referred to a "paralyzed fact." There was another old boy from West Texas who was engaging in a debate on the front and back mike with an erudite lawyer from Dallas one day in the House. This erudite lawyer was having difficulty understanding Mr. Bill Chambers. He said, "Mr. Bill, you've gone over that and over that, and I still don't understand what you're trying to do." Representative Chambers said, "Mr. Bergman, all I can tell you is it takes a lot of lather to shave a mule." I've never heard Bill Messer or Wilhelmina Delco or any of these other erudite legislators say that type of thing.

David Prindle: Last week I took my sixteen-month-old son to Barton Creek Mall. He's about twenty inches tall and he has a vocabulary of about twenty-five words, all of them except "mama" and "dada" of one syllable. I took him into a video parlor at the mall. Now, a video parlor is dark, has a lot of machines against the wall with red, green, and white flashing lights, all sorts of strange mechanical sounds, beeps and whorls. My son stood in the entrance for about thirty seconds gazing around, and then he took three running steps into the center of the room and went, "WOW!"

Until recently this was more or less the attitude of people when they thought about the Texas oil industry. Twenty-five years ago you had two hundred thousand wells in Texas.

You had an entire industry or a series complex of industries: drillers, salt water haulers, petrochemical industry, all that sort of thing, based upon, we thought, the oil and gas industries. When anyone from the Northeast would come down to Texas and start talking about it, the first thing they would do was go, "Wow, the oil industry!"

That's wrong. We know now that the oil industry is, of course, declining. We think Texas is declining because of it. That is, we know that Houston and Midland are becoming ghost towns. We know that the state treasury is being depleted very rapidly. We know that marginal wells are about to be placed on the endangered species list. All of this we think we know. I want to suggest that this image we have of "Texas, wow, the oil industry," is a fundamentally wrong way of thinking about the oil and gas industry in Texas history.

What has really happened over the past seventy or seventy-five years in the oil industry is that the legislature of the state and the Railroad Commission have managed the petroleum industry in a way to bring about the maximum prosperity to the state. They have done this for three objectives. They wanted to keep the price as high as economic circumstances would permit. They wanted to keep the money in Texas as opposed to seeing it migrate to New York. John Gunther in the forties said that Texas was the most valuable thing that New York owned. That is no longer true because the politicians of this state reversed the process. Third, the people in the legislature and the Railroad Commission wanted to spread the money around as equally and widely as possible within the state. The result was that by the sixties it was impossible to talk about Texas as a colonial appendage of Yankees.

Now, how did they do this? They did this, first of all, with market demand prorationing which suppressed the production of oil, thus providing a floor for the price. They did it with common carrier laws for pipelines, which forced pipeline companies to carry the oil of even small and unpowerful people. They did it with spacing and allocation rules which made for very many wells being drilled, owned by very many common people. In other words, as a summary, they favored Texas independent producers, drilling companies, work-over services, and the whole complex of the oil industry. The result was a more prosperous state and a state income which was more equally distributed.

My brief conclusion from all of this is that it has been not so much the occurrence of petroleum, but intelligent public policy that has been responsible for the prosperity of Texas in the past fifty years. And that's a paralyzed fact. A corollary to this is that at the moment, we do not have an oil price crisis in Texas. We have a public policy crisis. You don't need natural resources to be prosperous. New England now has the lowest unemployment rate of any region in the nation, and New England has no natural resources. New England is prosperous now because it has emphasized two things: education and a different way of collecting taxes than Texas has. I am forbidden to talk about the future, but I cannot refrain from pointing out that the reason New England is prosperous at the moment is because it has emphasized education. The other thing I want to point out is that Texas is the only large industrial state without a state income tax.

George Christian: More than likely, it will remain the only industrial state without an income tax.

Molly Ivins: I wanted to associate myself with a terribly profound thought that has lately been purveyed around the state by one of our better Republican gubernatorial candidates: "I do believe that Texas will always be Texas." This is the same gubernatorial candidate who thinks you get AIDS through your feet. But I find, not necessarily to my delight, that Texas changes very little at all.

The relationship between the economy and politics in this state seems to me best outlined by the relationship between the oil industry and the Railroad Commission, which I believe has been misstated here by both Mr. Messer and our good Professor who knows a great deal more about it than I do. The misstatement was very simple in both cases. The idea was that the Railroad Commission did the price fixing or that the Railroad Commission managed the industry for maximum profits. In fact, the industry managed the Railroad Commission, and that is the relationship between business and politics in this state.

In the good old days, before we had 100 per cent allowable, representatives of the seven majors would meet in a hotel room in Houston once a month and decide what the allowable would be. Then they would call Austin and tell the Railroad Commission, which would then announce it. It seems to me that that is still the way things work at the legislature. Business does run government.

I am always amused to hear businessmen like Mr. Louis Austin complain about regulations, the terrible, onerous burden of government regulation on business. It just breaks my heart every time I hear them talk about it. If you want to know how regulation is accomplished in the Texas Legislature, I will explain it to you. Representatives of business interests come to the legislature and beg to be regulated. This is precisely what happens. Year after year, the people who repair watches, the interior decorators, the people who install the lawn sprinklers, come to the legislature and say, "Please, please, we want government regulation." And that is how regulation works. It is done of, by, and for business in this state. Then of course when I hear businessmen complain about it, it just makes me terribly happy.

By the way, let me put in a plug. The legislature, for reasons totally unclear to me, has consistently refused to regulate interior decorators. There is an opportunity here that should not be overlooked. If we license the guys, we could put on riders forever outlawing lime-green shag carpeting, spackles in the ceiling and other offenses against humanity.

Every now and again, when you see an industry that is theoretically regulated, as were nursing homes in this state, a situation will become so appalling that the press will bestir itself and there will be some public outcry. Then, as in the case of nursing homes, the regulatory board which allegedly regulated that industry went through the most traumatic crisis, because of course all the members of the regulatory commission were bought and paid for and owned by the industry itself. Then you see what kind of hassle it takes to actually have a regulatory system that does some enforcement. That was a matter that took almost two whole sessions for the Texas Legislature. We finally made some progress on that.

It seems to me that in our state it almost literally requires a gory death to kick the Texas Legislature into action. Artesia Hall, the death of the child who was forced to swallow lye and then given no medical treatment for three days, was the history of how we started to regulate private church schools in this state. The nursing home case is more recent. But these are still very much the only ways that you can ever get anything done in the legislature. It's just a huge, public, stinking scandal.

The two most distinguishing features of the Texas Legislature as a body are that it is cheap and mean. It is a fascinating body in terms of the amount of bitching that one hears consistently about the outrageous expenditures on public welfare and people getting away with things. In the immortal words of one member, "The only thing to do with those people is to clip them and spay them: clip the men; spay the women." We are talking about a state that gives thirty-eight dollars a month per dependent child. A month. I think that's cheap and mean.

There is, however, a tradition of civility in the Texas Legislature that is really irresistible. It's the reason one becomes fond of that very peculiar institution. When I first started writing for the *Texas Observer* sixteen years ago, I would regularly denounce some miscreant in the legislature as one who ran on all fours and molested small children and had the brains of an adolescent pissant. And then it would occur to me after the paper had gone to bed that William Brann had been shot in the back for that kind of thing. But I would see my named miscreant in the halls of the legislature right after the paper came out, and the only response was, "Oh, baby, you put my name in your paper!" It is that tradition of civility that keeps one from total despair.

I do believe that the legislature is a representative body. It's one of Carl Parker's favorite sayings that if you took all the fools out of the legislature it would no longer be a representative body. However, I have always been of the opinion that the people of this state deserve better. I notice it was with some complacency Messer said that the small-town businessman had always identified with the richest guys in Dallas and Houston. I believe that's not true. I believe there is a deep streak of populism in this state that's always been there. It's a native political sentiment; it's not imported from the East. It's a genuine form of anger. What happens is that like any state with an establishment, the money goes on the side of the establishment. The people's votes do not avail much, in fact, even in a democratic system because, as we all know, the grease of politics is money.

I also wanted to address the idea that the Texas Legislature or Texas politics generically are somehow improving or are by no means as amusing as they used to be. "Texas will always be Texas." For years now people have been saying to me, "But isn't it getting better?" And I kind of go, "What better? Are you talking about Mike Martin? Are you talking about the Killer Bees?" If I have to look further for people who are funny, I look at the speaker's dais. Gib Lewis, the speaker, is one of my favorites. What a honey. He, in case y'all haven't heard, does have a solution to the state's budget problem. It's the Employee "Nutrition" Program. It's where you let them retire gradually and don't replace them.

The signal change that has occurred in the years I've been watching Texas politics is the rise of the Republican Party. I, like all right thinking people in this state, had for years thought how wonderful it would be to have a second political party. It would be just like our high school civics textbooks. There would be two political parties, and they'd both be progressive. There would be no corruption.

Wouldn't it be grand? Whoever would have imagined that some people would have started a political party *to the right* of Texas Democrats? How could they have thought of such a thing?

Cyndi Krier is a particularly attractive specimen of Republican, but don't let her fool you. They're not all like that. Warren Burnett, the great Texas attorney, always says, "You should never put anybody on a jury whose mouth puckers smaller than a chicken's asshole." And what we see in the legislature are all these mean-mouthed Republicans—very, very mean little mouths, and they're very angry all the time. I find them rather disconcerting, but I find after they've been around for a couple of sessions, by and large they loosen up and learn how to talk to their enemies.

I do want to assure you all that Texas politics as a source of amusement is as glorious as it ever was, in as fine form as it ever was, and indeed blooms daily with fresh wonders. Please keep paying attention.

Scott Bennett: George was going to present me as the conservative balance to Molly here, and I was going to thank him for polishing up my conservative credentials. I've certainly always thought of myself as a conservative, but you know the way trends go. I was the guest speaker at a Republican women's organization in Fort Worth not long ago. Speaking to such organizations is a real treat, for those of you who have never done that or been in one. The lady who was to introduce me beforehand said, "I always like to do introductions a bit different. Could you give me a couple of your political heroes?" And I said, "Well, okay, Allan Shivers and Dwight Eisenhower." And she looked positively puzzled. Later, when she got up to introduce me, she said, "Ladies, we have a very unusual guest here tonight, something you've never met before, a bona fide liberal." That is a true story. I was tempted to flee from the room.

At dinner the other night, I was talking to two friends of mine, both of whom suffer from not being native Texans. I was telling them I was going to be on this program and that the topic that George had recommended was the quality of business and political leadership in this state. The gentlemen at the table looked at me and said, "How can you tell the difference?" And, without blinking, the young lady said, "That's easy. If they have clout in Austin, they're businessmen, and if they're making money, they're politicians." Now that sounds like something Molly would have said, doesn't it? And if she had said it, I would have been terribly offended by it, as would Louis, probably, have been terribly offended by it because in truth I don't think that's true. In Texas today, I don't think anybody is making money.

The fact is that I do tend to agree with Molly that the business community, in some ecumenical manner, has had an enormous impact on the evolution of Texas. Where we disagree is that I think that's wonderful.

Now, why do I think that's wonderful? Well, I think it's wonderful because I think that the business community of this state, including names we're all familiar with, from Amon Carter in Fort Worth to Jesse Jones and George Brown in Houston, were men truly dedicated to working in the public realm to develop and to implement public policies that would serve the economic welfare of the state. It may have served the economic welfare of some somewhat better than others, but that's the way of the world. Overall, I think our state has done very well with the kind of leadership that people, whether they be businessmen or politicians such as Lyndon Johnson or Allan Shivers or John Connally, have brought to this state.

By the way, everyone who has moved into Texas from those wild lands up North comments to me that they are immediately astonished at the tremendous involvement in the political realm by businessmen. In fact, they're horrified by it. Hardly do they get moved in than someone's hit them up for a thousand-dollar fund-raiser, and, in this day and time, that's a little expensive. I don't think, John Odam, I've ever been to Houston that somebody didn't drag me to some cocktail party that was five hundred bucks for somebody roaming through the city of Houston from Lord knows where. Most of them have been from out of the state. You've noticed how they're all supporting oil for all that money you all gave them down there.

But in state, I think that we saw a group of people become involved because of a unique set of circumstances that really has not tended to exist in other states. One, we were a no-party state. I didn't say one-party state. I said no-party state, because as long as you called yourself a Democrat you could be anything on God's earth, and probably were. Business organizations weren't on the "outs" or on the "ins." We didn't see things like what happened at the end of Bill Clements's term when a group of long-dedicated business leaders and political leaders in Texas had been appointed to offices, and then a Democratic governor was elected, and the legislature recalled them. We had some skirmishes like that, but by and large, it was very easy for those in the business community to move from one camp to another, to be in the mainstream.

We've also heard other reasons touched on. For example, the business community in this state was able to harness the support of the yahoo element of this state by being their defenders against the North, and trying to overcome the colonial status that Texas for so long enjoyed. I think that this allowed the business establishment to maintain a relationship with the grass-roots voters that you didn't often find in other places.

I think they did a good job, and I think they did a good job because they were not ideological. These were pragmatic people. If they were conservative, I think they were conservative in the sense that they wanted a slow and deliberate social evolution. I think they wanted to develop a set of public policies that would result in a strong business sector. We have heard some of those policies described. They understood the need to invest in roads because we were a big state. We were a rural-oriented state. We had to have one of the finest road systems in the United States. We built it. Later on, we began to understand that education was extremely important. People like Allan Shivers and John

Connally stood forth strongly on the issue of education, on the need to begin to prepare for the future.

There are those who have criticized Lyndon Johnson, saying that he worked very hard to help those such as Brown and Root get contracts. Well, what did that do? It built a dam. It built roads, and those things were good for Texas. We sit in one of the most vibrant areas of this country today because a dam was built that brought power to the Hill Country of Texas. That is using public money to benefit private individuals. That is a role of government pragmatism, government for conservative ends, and that has served this state extremely well. The quality of the leadership in our business community, in our political community, was very high. It understood that public policy could be used to further the public good, not just of the rich and the powerful but of all people. The results that we've seen throughout the state, but especially in this area right here, were the results of the kind of policies that Lyndon Johnson and others strongly supported.

Now, there are some failures of business leadership in this state. One is in the realm of business, oddly enough. It's been awfully easy, over the years, to make money in oil in this state. You had to drill a lot of wells, but in the early days you didn't have to drill that many before you hit one. Yes, it took a certain level of expertise, but it was a matter that we've kept on keeping on, when probably we needed to begin to look at new industries and to make the kinds of private investments in those new industries that were necessary. We probably needed to begin adjusting our public policy to allow for the types of financial institutions necessary to build new industries to meet the future. The business leadership of the state has hoped to squeeze a few more good years out of what was, instead of looking at what's going to inevitably be.

Another problem of the business community here is that sometimes it's a little too practical for its own good. It's great to build great educational institutions that teach people how to earn a living. It's great to have engineering schools. It's great to have business schools, but there is an intellectual dimension to life—whether it be philosophy, whether it be history—that's important. It is important that people know how to think, not just to manage; that they know how to lead, not just to manage. I think that's a lot of what the Lyndon Johnson School is all about, teaching people to think, teaching people to lead—the intellectual dimension of life. You know, Texans are very fond of kicking Harvard and Yale around, of saying, "Well, gosh, these guys have imposed all sorts of policies on this country," and "the East Coast dominates the policy-making machinery of this country." Whether those policies have been good, bad, or indifferent, if the East Coast has dominated, it has done so because it has had no competition. We did not make the investment. We did not put the emphasis on things intellectual, on ideas and on policies. We were content to rely on very gifted politicians, with a great tradition of horse trading, to go to Washington or to go to Austin and try and deal with these matters. By the time legislation reaches the floor of the House, the battle is all but over. Where the battle begins is the battle for ideas that is fought every day, in the newspapers and the journals and the institutions of this country. Too often the business community of Texas has not put its money in this direction.

The third criticism I would have of business leadership in this state is an inclination to often fall into what I would call typical chamber of commerce boosterism. Everything is great here. There's nothing wrong with this place. Texas is not the new Jerusalem. It may be closer to it than New York City, but it's not there. I don't think that any great purpose is served by a business community that continually wants to circle the wagons, continually wants to say, "Everything's great in our city." I don't think this is quite so true on the state level as it has been. Dallas was once probably the worst about saying, "We don't have any problems here," and going hammer and tongs to fight any type of criticism, no matter how constructive it's intended. These do a disservice to themselves and to their local communities.

One of my concerns is over the evolution of a two-party system. Although a lifelong Republican, I greet this development in Texas with great apprehension for several reasons. One is that we find more and more of those who participate in the day-in, day-out activities of the political parties to be more extreme in their philosophies. The more the extremists become involved, the more the mainstream, whether it be the liberal mainstream or the conservative mainstream, opt out. Therefore, we find that the choices that stand before us in the fall have been determined by a very narrow band of people with very narrow agendas, months before.

I'm also somewhat concerned in that as the Republican Party comes to power, it is a party lacking in depth. That's not quite the criticism it sounds like. The fact is that if you're going to draw congressmen, you're most likely to draw those congressmen from officeholders at the legislative level or at the county commissioner level or whatever. Republicans simply haven't had many of those offices. So the depth from which to draw is not very good. Sometimes they get lucky. A Cyndi Krier comes along and they find a really eloquent and open-minded and capable representative. I'm afraid, Cyndi, that you remain one of the exceptions.

The other thing that concerns me is that we constantly hear talk of bringing the Reagan Revolution to Texas, and we hear talk like, "You have to cut back government. You have to cut taxes. You have to reduce regulation." Well, we had the Reagan Revolution in Texas a hundred and fifty years ago, and it's been going forward ever since. I fear many of my Republican friends have missed the fourth tenet of the Reagan Revolution, which is states' responsibilities. President Reagan has spent a great deal of time saying that states have a place in our federal system, a very important role in our federal system, and they must meet those responsibilities. Perhaps he has forgotten that one of the reasons so much power gravitated to Washington was because states were failing to meet those responsibilities. Now they're being turned back here, and I don't know that you always meet those responsiblities with less government. What is too much government at the federal level may not be too much government at the state level. This is where the responsibility of education lies, of basic infrastructure lies, the foundation on which the economy of this state must be built. Very wise business leaders and their partners in public life in Texas for decades have understood that partnership. I hope that we can continue to understand it in the future.

George Christian: In our remaining moments, I might mention some of the things we haven't covered that are awfully important to this state. We barely mentioned one of them.

We didn't cover the PSF and the PUF and the PAC. That's the Permanent School Fund, the Permanent University Fund, and the political action committee. I think all of those have had tremendous impact on this state, on the progress of this state. You might get some quarrels about that in relation to the PAC, but certainly the first two.

We barely mentioned the pay-as-you-go amendment to the Texas Constitution, which was passed in the forties to prevent this state from going into the red on operating costs as it did during the dismal thirties. Most of the states now have adopted pay-as-you-go. In Texas it has meant innumerable tax fights over the last forty years. We've had some troubles with pay-as-you-go, but since we don't have the luxury of borrowing for operating costs, it has created what we like to refer to as "fiscal responsibility." Molly might disagree with that term, but it is commonly used. We have it in Texas.

We barely mentioned the good roads program in Texas, which was a constitutional amendment in the forties that said we're going to have a transportation system to tie the rural and urban areas of this state together and to give us access to markets in Mexico, which had not opened up until the thirties mainly because of lack of transportation.

We didn't talk too much about the business-driven reforms in this state over the past fifty years. At the outset Fred Hartman in the audience over here mentioned the prison reforms of 1947. Nobody now can remember what shape we were in in our prison system prior to that. There were the mental health reforms of the late forties and early fifties. We've done an awful lot with this business-dominated legislature, which I think all of us agree probably exists.

We didn't really get into the fact, beyond mentioning Ross Perot and the latest school reforms, that in the late forties another business-driven reform, the Gilmer-Aiken Program, changed the entire structure of public schools in this state, I think for the better.

In closing, I'd just like to ask any of the panelists to comment on anything that's been said by other panelists or raise any subject you might like to raise.

Bill Messer: I want to comment on one thing and agree in part with what Molly said on one aspect. She said there's a strong populism trend in Texas, and that's right. It's what T. R. Fehrenbach calls "folk conservatism," though, because it's not liberal populism. The hero of initiative and referendum was Bill Clements. There are populists in the Republican Party, just like in the Democratic Party, and it basically comes from that us-against-them attitude that we inherited from our forebears. I think there is a commonality of interest, though, between the department store owner and the big businessman. The big businessman in Texas is the head of a bank holding company, and if you take all of the bank holding companies in Texas, they're not as big as CitiBank in New York. It's the independent oilman like Hunt, who's not as big as Exxon or somebody else. I think there is that commonality of interest, and that is why you have populism or folk conservatism that runs through both parties and runs through politics in Texas and will continue to for some time to come.

Scott Bennett: My favorite line from one of Molly's past columns was that "if there were no progressive businessmen in Texas, there would be no progressives at all." That is one of her most astute observations.

George Christian: Molly, I'm not going to give you the last word, so you chime in right now.

Molly Ivins: Well, in fact I was about to use that very line, one of my classic observations that in fact was inspired by Ross Perot. Mr. Bennett had said at one point in the Texas Legislature they wanted slow and deliberated social evolution. I am afraid that is a serious misrepresentation of the position of the legislature, at least as far as race relations are concerned. They did not want slow and deliberated evolution. They wanted no change at all and made that emphatically clear for a very long and dreary period of this state's history.

George Christian: I will add that we were still passing segregation laws as recently as 1957, so I agree with that. But I'll also point out again, regarding populism in Texas, which is an old political movement, it was also over virtually its entire life a very racist political movement.

Cyndi, do you have anything to add?

Cyndi Taylor Krier: Just that in the past, business and oil have almost been synonymous, and when we talk so much about the diversification of our state's economy in the future, you may see a diversification of business interests that could dramatically impact on the political structure.

George Christian: David Prindle, you tell us the oil price is going up and we'll wind this thing down.

David Prindle: It is going up.

George Christian: Thank you all for your kind attention.

TEXAS TOMORROW

THE CHALLENGES AHEAD

Max Sherman: As we move from the topics of change, chaos and culture, back through the worlds of politics and the economy into the Texas of tomorrow, let me share three thoughts by way of introduction. As we listened to the panels this morning, there was one constant ingredient—the ingredient of diversity: geographic, ethnic, economic; large cities and small towns, rivers, bays, estuaries, dams, dry rivers and active rivers traversing hundreds of miles of the state of Texas. One symbol of the state's diversity is a series of publications by the Institute of Texan Cultures entitled *Texians and Texans.* The series covers a whole range of Texans: Czechs, French, Indians, Germans, Norwegians, Mexicans, Poles, Spaniards, and Italians. It's this diversity that gives Texas its unique heritage, but it's also part of our challenge.

As we seek a perspective for the future, let me call your attention to a wonderful book by Reagan Bradshaw and Griffin Smith published by Texas Monthly Press—*The Forgotten Texas: A Wilderness Portfolio.* In a section on Capote Falls, the reader is reminded that: "Although the past of Capote Falls is measured in centuries, its future may be measured in years." Unless we do what our speakers suggest and we start planning for the future of Texas, we may not have this very rich endowment that has caused us to be where we are today. We may very well be in the position of the man who said, "When I was little my father took me for a ride on a train before they all disappeared. I'll have to take my child for a ride on a river."

One other crisis in the seventies occurred when the oil and gas industry was not able to respond to the need in this country. I recall a newspaper account of an oil boom town that had gone bust. The interviewer had talked to several old-timers in the town; he talked to one old gentleman who was eighty. The fellow said that if he had known he was going to live so long, he would have taken better care of himself when he was younger. That's essentially where we are.

The third point comes out of something that was said this morning. More than twenty years ago, President and Mrs. Johnson dreamed of a school where future leaders could be trained. The dream was cultivated, and through hard work and the marshaling of resources, the dream became a reality. Today graduates of the LBJ School are just moving into leadership roles not only in Texas but throughout the nation. It shows what can be done with long-range planning, a lot of hard work, and the kinds of things that we are looking at in this forum.

So let these ideas be reminders to all of us to do what our panelists this morning suggested: to let our imaginations wander, to maintain that Texas spirit that sustains us in our quest to be larger than life, and to maintain this landscape we all call Texas.

Dave McNeely: This morning we took a look in a couple of panels at how we got where we are. Now we look at where we go from here. So all you stockbrokers listen up and get up in the front row. We've timed this to coincide with the closing of the New York market so that you won't get too big a jump.

Sometimes in Texas we confuse cause and effect. I'm reminded of the fellow whose eyeballs protruded very seriously, a condition he had had for quite some time. He became so despondent that he went to a haberdasher to buy a new set of clothes so that he could do himself up in style. When he walked in, the clerk looked at him and said, "Well, let's see, what do you need?" And he said, "I need a whole new set of clothes from head to toe." "Well, fine," the clerk said, "looks like about a six and seven-eighths hat; shirt'll be fifteen-and-a-half, thirty-three; waist looks like about a thirty-four; pants, thirty-one-inch inseam; size nine-and-a-half B shoes." And the fellow said, "Well, that's wonderful. I've never seen anybody do anything like that before. Everything is correct except the shirt size. You had me wearing a fifteen-and-a-half, thirty-three, and I wear a fifteen, thirty-three." Then the clerk said, "Well, you can do that if you want, but it'll make your eyes bug out."

From a political vantage point, we've had some of the same situations in this state for the last fifteen years or so. We've been floating on a lot of oil, and we've got a familiar refrain: "No new taxes, no new taxes, no income tax." It reminds me of a group of chickens who think they can walk on water. They've gotten used to saying "No webbed feet, no webbed feet, we don't need webbed feet." Now with the oil prices going down, and the oil coating getting thinner and thinner, we are going to have either some webbed feet or some wet chickens.

Bernard Weinstein: Recent months have seen the development of a new national sport called Texas-bashing. It's become very, very popular, and the national media are filled with articles that are less than complimentary about our state. Just about the best of those appears in the current issue of *The New Republic,* and it's called "Let Them Rot in the Sun." I'll just read one sentence from that article. " 'Oil recession plunges Houston into state of mental depression,' says *The Wall Street Journal.* Good, say I. All the reports of economic catastrophe in America's oil regions fill me with unwholesome glee." And it gets better. Another piece appeared in the *Chicago Tribune* and was reprinted in the *Dallas Morning News* a couple of days ago, and I want to read a couple of paragraphs from this piece by Bill Neikirk.

> Sorry, J.R., but I don't want to bail out Dallas. Since I was a boy listening to the radio, I have heard Texas oil men and fundamentalist ministers and self-righteous officials preach the virtues of free enterprise and unfettered capitalism. The free market, they said, was the closest thing to godliness. It wasn't until years later that I realized the Texas economy has long existed on artificially controlled oil prices, not free enterprise. It was all a gigantic hoax. Texas profited enormously when OPEC raised its prices while we waited bleary-eyed in long gasoline lines. The oil boom lured people and income from the frost belt, and you, you laughed at we poor, suffering snow-shovelers. "Freeze a Yankee," you said, as you drove around in your gas guzzlers.

Now, there's a lot of truth in that statement. I don't like to read it; I don't like to repeat it. But I think he's right on when he talks about the true basis of prosperity in Texas during the seventies and early eighties.

It wasn't just oil, it was rising commodity prices generally. We tend to focus on the energy business, but that was an inflationary decade, and the price of wheat and soybeans and pork bellies and everything else was going up. Agriculture is our second biggest industry in the state. So that inflationary decade of rising commodity prices pumped a lot of income into the state, and that in turn generated a fair amount of economic growth. You can look at personal income growth, or state production. But what we didn't have a lot of in the seventies and early eighties was economic development, and I believe there's a fundamental difference between economic growth and economic development. Economic growth is something that happens to you; economic development is something you do for yourself.

The recent history of Texas is one whereby we have been the beneficiary of forces that were pretty much beyond our control. OPEC and inflation are the most recent examples of that, but one can go back further and point to other political and economic developments that really helped us. Now we're on the other side of that phenomenon. As commodity prices fall, and as that hits our agricultural and our energy sectors, it shows us how vulnerable we are.

What we obviously need in the state of Texas in the future is more economic development. The real difference between Texas's past and Texas's future is that we're going to have to work harder, and we're going to have to work smarter, and we're going to have to be truly entrepreneurial. One of the great myths about Texas is that we are an entrepreneurial place. Some of the evidence is not very encouraging on that score. If you look at the number of new business starts in the state, it's been dropping for the last three years, while it's been rising enormously in places like California and Massachusetts. The next several years will be a true test of how entrepreneurial we are. It was easy to be an entrepreneur when commodity prices were rising. It was easy to make money. The new entrepreneurship is going to require a different set of attitudes and attributes, changes in the way we regulate, changes in the way we do business, changes in the way we attract and accumulate capital.

There is going to be a fundamental difference in the years ahead in terms of some demographics. I disagree a bit with Mayor Cisneros and some of his prognostications. I don't think Texas is going to be growing very fast over the next fifteen years. In 1986 we may well see zero net migration to the state. Migration to Texas has dropped tremendously in recent years. In 1982 three hundred thousand more people moved into the state than moved out of the state. Last year it was thirty thousand; that's a 90 per cent drop. I think this year it's going to be flat. The upper Texas Gulf Coast is probably going to have eighty or ninety thousand more people moving out than moving in this year. Migration has been the primary source of our population growth, and that's going to be flat for the next fifteen years. I don't think that has a lot to do with economic circumstances but more with some fundamental demographic changes: the aging of the U.S. population; the fact that there are fewer people entering the work force every year.

So against this backdrop, what do we do? If we're not going to have this migration stream, what other types of policies or strategies might we be thinking of? I'm not going to go into any detail, but let me just mention three or four things. Number one, I think the oil card has been played. I don't care what happens to oil prices. Twenty-five-dollar oil is not going to do very much for the Texas economy. Twenty-five-dollar oil is not going to refuel a drilling boom. Oil is just another commodity; it is not going to be the source of employment and income growth in our future under any conceivable scenario. So we've got to put that one aside. What we need to focus on in terms of economic development is more of an internally focused, grass-roots strategy, where we really look at our strengths and our weaknesses and we deal forthrightly with our weaknesses. Most important, we need to continue to focus on upgrading Texas's human capital.

People often ask me, what are going to be the future industries of Texas? What should we be targeting? And I say, I don't know. I don't know whether the electronic widget industry is where the future of Texas lies. But I do know whatever that future is, we're more likely to achieve it if we have a functionally literate work force, if we have people who can read and write and compute and analyze. If we can take care of that human infrastructure, economic development will take care of itself.

There are a couple of other things that we can do. At the state level there aren't a lot of buttons we can push, but there are a few that we can push to try to improve the economic and business climate in this state, and I'll end by just suggesting one or two. Certainly, deregulation. Despite the lip service we pay to free enterprise, we are an over-regulated state, particularly financial institutions and transportation. The second thing that we really need to do is overhaul our tax system. That doesn't necessarily mean an income tax, but it means trying to develop a tax system that is more balanced and that is more in sync with changes in the state's economy. And then the final thing we need to do is really encourage entrepreneurship and leadership in this state. I think those are the real keys to economic development.

Jim Hightower: I'm honored to be a participant in this sesquicentennial dialogue and high-level hog-calling contest, which I guess is pretty much what it gets down to. I can imagine that a good number of y'all, when you prepare to hear a discourse on agriculture, have your eyes glaze over and your mind disengage entirely. But like that old bumper sticker says, "If you eat, you're involved in agriculture." I'm sitting here looking out at you, and some of you have been getting real involved, from what I'm seeing here. Ray Marshall has been packing away the groceries, right down here in the front row. We really all have to get involved in the shaping of some new agricultural policies in this state and in this country, not merely to save a few family farmers and ranchers, but primarily because their enterprise can be a major salvation for the overall Texas economy.

It's kind of popular these days to assume that the family farm, the family ranch, is a doomed creature, and some even pontificate that, well, our agricultural production is going to shift into the hands of Japanese managers, producing the world's staple crops on high-tech, low-wage plantations in Brazil and other host countries. A more common view offered by such visionaries as Earl Butz is that the productive assets of American agriculture will shift rather quickly and inevitably from the hands of independent family entrepreneurs into the control of U.S.-based conglomerates, sort of a "star wars" concept of integrated management combines that envelop and direct an agriculture that is industrialized, that is centralized and that is monopolized. The only ones in bib overalls are out there on the tractors as contract producers, really, under people wearing three-piece suits.

Well, I think they're nuts. I don't think it is either good or permissible economic policy to destroy the efficiency and the competitiveness of the existing family farm structure of agriculture and to put America's food future into the hands of either foreign or conglomerate interests. Rather, we should be adjusting our policies, our technologies, our strategies, our systems and our bureaucracies to fit the productive needs of America's most efficient and most competitive economic unit, which is that independent family farm or ranch.

By no means am I arguing to you that we should just keep on keeping on with the same old ways of agriculture. I am arguing that we ought to base a new, more sophisticated, market-sensitive agriculture on the very people who have consistently proven their value to our economy, by which I mean that dirt farmer and hardscrabble rancher out there. By just planting a few new seeds of agricultural development and nurturing them properly in the next several years, we can revitalize family farm agriculture in this state.

Among those seeds is aggressive direct marketing by the farmers themselves, direct domestically, direct internationally; extensive diversification of our agricultural production, and the expansion by farmers in joint ventures with small companies into value-added agricultural enterprises. This requires no wrenching of our economy, no heavy hand of government and no artificial tampering with that magic of the marketplace, as El Presidente spoke of in his last State of the Union Address. Rather, it requires a common-sense realization that our most fertile prospect for true economic diversity and growth is our own enterprising people.

Instead of kissing off these people, saying "Adios, chump" to them, we could instead be helping them shift production into a variety of staples and specialty crops that do return profitable prices to the farmer. We can be finding new markets for that production, helping those farmers and ranchers sell it directly to domestic and foreign buyers, and we can encourage those people to become the processors of the commodities that they produce. What we get back as a public, if we do this, is billions of dollars in grass-roots economic development. Allow me just one statistic to give you an example of this latter point. Texas now processes only 6 per cent of the nation's food. If we were to increase that even to 7 per cent, that would add a billion dollars to our economy, a billion dollars in direct sales, not counting the ripple effect of that wealth.

We're not talking about some pie-in-the-sky scheme here, some economist's wet dream of what might be, but rather about a realistic future of economic growth, economic development, if Bernard insists on that, that we can reach in a very short time and toward which we are already moving in the state of Texas. We at the Department of Agriculture, working with the legislature, working with Texas A&M and other institutions, have indeed assisted in the launching of several successful agricultural enterprises that head us off in this direction.

Rather than wax eloquent about specific projects, let me instead just offer you a description of what a typical Texas farm might look like five, ten, fifteen years down the road if we pursue directions that are already under way. Consider an East Texas farm, a full-time commercial operation. It still is a mid-size operation out there, maybe on the order of four or five hundred acres. It's still run by the family. Spud and Eula and the kids and Elmer are the ones out there doing the work on it. But they're not trying to make a go of it just by raising cattle and hay and a little bit of yams. Instead they have diversified dramatically. They do have cattle, but it's a herd of one of the special lean cuisine breeds, with calves that have been produced through inexpensive embryo transplant techniques. The beef from this operation is slaughtered and packed at a regional cooperatively owned facility. It is labeled with a certified Taste-of-Texas logo, not only for marketing in supermarkets but also direct marketing, sold under advance-marketing contracts to nutrition-conscious consumers.

They might have another forty acres that's set aside in blueberries. These blueberries are produced under drip irrigation and delivered by airlift in the springtime at premium prices to East Coast markets. Texas can supply them three weeks ahead of other states, with later blueberry production going into southwestern and California markets, and a reserve of blueberry production being used for processing into a line of jams, into Blueberry Newtons, into freeze-dried and frozen blueberries in the state.

We might put another forty acres into Christmas trees and supply a fragrant, fresh, top-quality inexpensive tree to Texans who previously had been paying twice as much for a Montana product that dropped half its needles before Santa came down the chimney.

We've got another forty acres in specialty crops, which might include such boutique items as onions sold by mail order, broccoli and cauliflower marketed direct to Dallas restaurants for salad bar use, Oriental vegetables to supply the burgeoning Asian-American population in Houston and in Dallas. A greenhouse enterprise could be added into it, developing native Texas landscape plants, produced by clone technology. The greenhouse enterprise also might be involved in production of fresh sprouts and culinary herbs, which are packaged on the farm and marketed under a family label direct to contract customers in Tyler and Longview and Marshall.

Then there might be a fishpond, or two or three fishponds, on that farm, producing crawfish and redfish for area restaurants, and game fish for stocking local lakes. Some of the ponds would use algae to cover the pond as a source of food for the fish. But this algae is also a fast-growing, very high-protein product, so it is harvested almost daily, dried and fed to the cattle.

We can go on and on with this picture. There's no limit to what can be done, and my point is it is being done right now:

pinto bean production, 99.9 per cent of which comes out of Colorado right now; varietal grapes, we're going to have a major grape industry in this state. It's not all Chateau Bubba that we're making, either. We're making some very good wines. New crops, like amaranth down in Southwest Texas, a high-protein grain product; kenaf, down in the Rio Grande, out of which we manufacture newsprint; natural beef production, again, no limit.

But my point is that progressive family enterprises can do all of this, generating wealth not only for themselves but also for their local economy. Everything mentioned here already is being developed in the state of Texas. It is our future, and it is a future that is based on our people. I agree that what we must have is economic development in the state of Texas, an intentional program of economic development. But it's important that we decide economic development for whom and by whom. Texas did not get where it is by waiting on Toyota to come build an auto plant to save our economy in the state of Texas. Rather we invested in our own people, and that's what we must do again. Rather than calling on outside conglomerates to take over this economy, we can be making an aggressive, concerted effort to invest in our own people to build that prosperous future at the grass roots, nurturing the growth of these home-grown enterprises. It's the opposite of what that guy in the White House says about trickle-down theory of economic growth. Instead, we're talking about percolate up. It is a healthy economy that comes out of that.

Meg Wilson: Technology is an area that is of critical importance to us, and it's something that's only good if it's used. Its use is inevitable. We've got two billion years of history that says that. Getting into the recent past, the director of the patent office at the beginning of the century said once, "Everything that could be invented has been invented." He was wrong, obviously. Another statement at a critical point in our nation's history was this: "The phone is a wonderful invention. Every town may have one someday." I think it's obvious that Texas knows how to use technology, as evidenced by what Jim has just said. We have successfully exploited our agricultural research, and our research in energy production, so that we are the best in the world in some of what we do in that area.

The transition that Texas is going through is giving this state an incredible opportunity to be great again, or remain great, depending on your perspective, through achievements that we've never been known for. The pain of the current transition, the economic dislocation that we're currently going through, will be a temporary problem if we can capitalize on the critical mass that is building. It will allow us to leap ahead in areas that can make the state great, and help in rebuilding not just the state's, but the nation's competitive position.

Some people say that Texas has succeeded purely by luck. Some say that it's a two-legged stool, standing on legs of agriculture and petroleum. Others say that it resembles a third world country, rich in raw materials that are shipped out, processed, and returned for sale. So, are we a third world economy, standing on two legs and out of luck? No. It's going to take a lot of hard work to position ourselves to be prosperous into the twenty-first century. The critical period for the efforts to reach that prosperity will be in the next four to six years. We are on the brink of positive changes in legislative policy, academic achievement, business development, human resource development, and regional cooperation.

Technology development is a key to many of these changes, sometimes as an input, as an output, or as a catalyst. In the area of legislative consensus, for instance, I think we are at a turning point of seeing a change in philosophy. The legislature is now going to be able to see some expenditures as investments instead of only as expenditures. That is evidenced by statements from the speaker, the lieutenant governor, and the governor, in looking at what we may do, for instance, with Outer Continental Shelf money. We can use that to make an investment in our future. There is a common goal developing that we have to support our R and D base as an important part of our future development. There is a keen interest among House and Senate members, and in the last legislative session a resolution, a very simple, quiet little resolution, was passed which marked a major change in state policy. That resolution said, quietly and simply, that research and development are a critical part of our academic teaching function. That was a change in policy.

Last session the thirty-five-million-dollar advanced technology research program was passed. That was an investment, and it's an investment that we need to continue, because as we make those investments now, we may be reducing costs in the future when we may have even fewer revenues from traditional sources than we do now. How far we go depends on our strength in our universities, and we're not in the best position right now. I'm a cynical optimist. The cynical side says that we should be better than we are. We have exactly one department in the state of Texas that's number one in the nation; it's botany at UT. We should be better than that. We should have more in the top ten; we should have more that are one; we should have more that are two. We don't, because we have not made the investment in research and development, and our academic strength in the past has not been sufficient for the size and the nature of this state.

In the area of human resource development, we have a tradition of strong people, strong men and women. We will develop models for egalitarian economic participation if trends in the private sector and public sector continue that have been established in the last several years. These trends are evidenced by the growth of groups like TAME, the Texas Alliance for Minorities in Engineering, and by the interest in women that appears in a proposed minorities engineering scholarship bill. Over the next four years, there may be a concentrated effort to apply the best technologies to manufacturing development in the Valley, to establish competitive, productive companies, serving a growing regional market on both sides of the border as well as a national market. It will concentrate on adding value to local products.

In the area of regional cooperation, Texas is building models of regional cooperation which will be a legacy of the eighties, because only through such efforts can we marshal the resources to gain the critical mass, to create the greatness that we want. We have a problem of geographic proximity in this state that other areas don't have. Because of that we need new models of regional cooperation to make up for the great distances that we have to cross. One example of such a model is the High Technology Development Mayors' Task Force—Dallas and Fort Worth, working together to develop the Metroplex area.

We have, in Houston, the Houston Space Commercialization Center proposal which was just submitted to NASA, with Southwest Research of San Antonio being the lead organization. There's the Houston Area Research Center, a consortium of the University of Texas, A&M, Rice, and the University of Houston, working together for technology development and technology applications and transfer.

There is the Austin-San Antonio Corridor; there is San Antonio's Biotechnology Research Park, which is an incredible effort put together through private and public cooperation. And, of course, we have the example that is so often cited of MCC, which was primarily a private sector initiative helped by public sector participation.

There are pitfalls in all of this. We can't proceed in developing an economy based on value-added and manufacturing, aerospace commercialization, routine use of biotechnology, et cetera, without offering all of our participants in our economy the tools to develop all of their resources.

By improving our educational system, we can avoid the worst manifestations of what is sometimes called the pink-collar ghetto, a severely stratified manufacturing work force and minority unemployment. We have to see evolution of capital in its use and its applications. We have to learn how to direct the flow toward longer-term, high-risk deals. The technical risk in some of these projects is no greater than an oil well, but when time—not a year, but five years—is combined with technical risk, it seems threatening to Texans who otherwise are famous for taking risks. If they can learn what that means, that that risk is something they can get past, we can develop the entrepreneurial base that Bernard Weinstein is talking about. It's going to have to be an evolutionary process, not a revolutionary process, because we have to bring along the capital base, the human base; we have to create the entrepreneurs and the managers. The managers are sometimes called free radicals, in the scientific sense. We are missing those in Texas. That's what they have in Massachusetts's Loop 128; that's what they have in Silicon Valley.

We have a future to build in this state, if we'll build on our education base, build on our technology base. It's one that will be successful for this state. It will help us in economic development, because technology is not just something for creating new industries. It is also what we apply to our old industries. It is something that will be infused into our entire society. If we learn how to take advantage of it, we will have a strong, prosperous economy.

Earl Lewis: At a forum where one of the interests has to be our history and our traditions, I think the thing I'd like to do and escape alive from the room is to suggest that we ought to abandon two of our most cherished Texas traditions in order to enhance the prospects that we will go into the future with a quality of life available to the generality of our people, which is not true as we sit here this afternoon.

I think we've got to abandon our faithfulness to a tradition that involves the preservation and development of inadequate human care and human development services. We are richly distinguished for the paucity of our resources that we have historically invested in the development of personal strengths of various kinds in the people of the state. And that tradition I recommend that we abandon very, very completely. We have large socio-economic disparities among Texans that we all are aware of. Those disparities are not confined to our traditional ethnic minorities, but a very, very large sector of the population of this state is comprised of Hispanics and black people, who have historically been handicapped, to put it euphemistically, by an assortment of deprivations, not all of which were accidental.

It looks as though we're going to have a large increase in the fraction of Texans in the future that will come from these two groups, which are currently and historically so underserved by a variety of our institutions. This poses an enormous challenge. One estimate suggests that by as early as the year 2000, which almost seems tomorrow, more than 50 per cent of the Texas young people under fifteen years of age will be Hispanic and black. And those numbers just suggest to me the enormity of the challenge of getting geared to provide developmental support for that large contingent of people.

The evidence that we have more than dragged our feet on the human development, care-for-the-human-being side is pretty overwhelming. In 1983, for example, we had in this state an 11.1 per cent rate of infant mortality. There were in that year twenty-eight states with lower infant mortality rates than Texas. That happened to have been a year when we were blessed by the comptroller's projection of nine hundred and fifty six million dollars in surplus in the treasury of the state. And if you can make a great deal of sense out of mixing those facts that I've just given you, you're much more skillful than I.

On the poverty front, in 1979 about 14.7 per cent of the population of this state were in poverty. Believe it or not, thirty-seven other states in the United States had lower poverty rates, and they were peopled by individuals who presumably breathe oxygen and dress probably one leg at a time. But here we were, with very handsome surpluses in this state, with a poverty level pegged at that scale and holding, if not in fact increasing. The welfare expenditures of the state were relatively very low. Thirty-seven states were investing more of their own internally generated revenue in public welfare programs, and that rate of investment exceeded ours in this state.

Then of course, there is the elementary and secondary education area. And I must be sure that I say two or three things positive, lest one say he just wallowed in the pathologies and the problems. The truth of the matter is the state has magnificent sectors of its past in many areas that it would take a long time to pay respect to, but consider my respect as having been paid here. One of the most recent phenomenal things that we did in the state was to adopt an extraordinary system of public education reform, truly extraordinary. It was most extraordinary because it was not selective about the way it addressed the educational needs of the young people of this state. It was uncommonly fair and responsible. It didn't seek to enhance the quality of education for middle-class white youngsters in the suburban enclaves of the state at the expense of large numbers of low-income Hispanic and black children in the urban centers of the state. It went right at the gut of the problem of inequity and injustice in this state, to all of our eternal credit, whether you wish to accept it or not.

But it was not long past when we were outspent in per person expenditures by forty-two states, as recently as 1982, 1983. Lest we think we've solved the problem, we do have extraordinary disparities in the amount of money that we still invest in the education of young people in the Texas system of public education. We're spending in the current year about $3,102.71 per pupil, and that's way up from where we have been. But among the 1,068 school districts in this state, there are some people spending a lovely $12,000 per year per pupil for operating and maintenance expenses, and there are some districts spending, believe it or not, below $1,800 a year in the current school year. That suggests that with as much progress as we made through House Bill 72, there are still enormous disparities still in place and entrenched.

The second abandonment that I'd like to suggest is that we give up some of our most cherished myths, the things that sometimes give us life and virility and vitality. These myths quite often distort the public discourse at the least and infect it with poison at the worst. They handicap us greatly in dealing with the common interests and needs of the people of the state as opposed to these fragmented interests that are giving us increasing skill in looking out after our individual interests and our group's interest and our single-issue pathology. John Gardner says there's no society in the world that has done better than we on the care for the individual's well-being. Where we have now to work hard is on those things that we have in common, and seek to address those.

One of these myths is that welfare in this country, public welfare, is a system through which the country really tries to help indigent, poor people, and it is primarily that or exclusively that. And that is simply hogwash. Our finest, deepest, richest system of public welfare is enjoyed by middle- and upper-class Americans in large abundance. Lest someone give me too much credit for this, let me suggest that you look at a little book with the marvelously appropriate title, *Time for Truth.* It's by William Simon. Mr. Simon is a very distinguished, and I hasten to add, very conservative and very successful American. In *Time for Truth,* he suggests that one of our biggest challenges is to take the middle class in this country off the dole. That's an enormous challenge for those of us in Texas, and if we give up the myth about who's on and who's not on welfare, I think it might be helpful.

Second, I think it would be helpful if we tried to back away from the notion that in this marvelous country, our government is really our problem. Amid all of the escalating complexities, the conflicts, the competition, and the interdependencies, we will need a rich mixture of governmental and other kinds of private initiatives to deal with the problems. It would be so regrettable and regressive to count the government out of the system.

Third, I think we need to lose some, not all, of the respect for the sanctity and purity of market forces, those lovely things that allocate rewards proportionately to people as they contribute to economic productivity and achievement, and things that if tampered with will just cause all kinds of misery for virtually everybody. I think we ought not to give up on the economists a hundred per cent, but it might be helpful to start in that direction.

Finally, it would be helpful as we try to go to this new day in Texas to give up the mythology that a rising tide floats all boats. What probably will float most of the boats is a high-quality, equitable system of education from the pre-kindergarten program to post-doctoral programs, all along. I have encountered in recent months people who are convinced that we can fix our future, contrary to Professor Weinstein's suggestion, if we can get enough brilliant people in our labs to produce the kinds of things that our industry can pounce on. Education is going to be essential to get Texans, all of us, to the table of rewards and benefits. It's also essential to give us what we need to contribute to the generality of the welfare of the state.

I think we have an enormous challenge in Texas, switching from our previous concerns to this human development thrust. It won't be easy for us, because we have not labored in this area long. I hope that we can do it. Arnold Toynbee, you know, in that terribly long study of history of his, talked about how the best societies often develop out of contests with the most serious challenges. I think this one is the one for us: to go for broke on the most precious resource in the world, the human being.

Annette Strauss: This morning's panelists illustrate how life in Texas has undergone a great change, both culturally and economically. This of course has greatly affected how municipal governments seek to protect and improve their own local quality of life. Governance today is really far removed from that of yesterday, when only the most essential services were addressed, and a very limited regulatory role was assumed.

As a member of the Dallas city council, I am most familiar

with the workings of the council-manager form of municipal administration and the challenges facing metropolitan north central Texas. So as I endeavor to discuss with you the shape of Texas's future, please be aware of some unavoidable local bias on my part.

Like other city governments in Texas, Dallas is now feeling the full force of the shock waves resulting from the turmoil of our regional economy and the withdrawal of federal participation in our social service programs. Right now our city budgets do remain balanced. Most of our bond ratings remain high, and thus far we have managed to meet the demands of existing municipal services. But things are changing very rapidly. The jury is still out on whether those of us in metropolitan municipal administration can turn the threat of service cutbacks, or great tax increases, into a challenge to the collective, creative talent of city government, to be able to adjust to these and to any further unanticipated changes in the economic landscape.

A brief reflection on the past twenty years reminds us that Texas cities from the late fifties through the seventies, fueled by very healthy local economies and seemingly limitless revenue pools, were able to supplement promotion by their own chambers of commerce with virtually skeletal administrative responsibilities. An aggressive expansion of federal jurisdiction over social services left our municipal leaders the very happy job of applying icing to the cake, with programs which sought to enhance our local cultural horizons, such as library inventories, neighborhood recreation facilities, and fine arts partnerships with the private sector.

With booming growth, however, in many instances the tested formulas of city management through regular bond programs and annual line-item budgeting became insufficient to deal with the broad range of new and very complex issues. It became increasingly clear that if our much-heralded pro-business climate were to remain intact, city administrators would have to begin utilizing the tools of corporate development, including state-of the-art data collection, revenue needs forecasting, and comprehensive intergovernmental planning.

While state and local leaders went about dividing the pie of economic expansion, initial forays into long-term planning for land use, transportation, criminal justice and upkeep of the infrastructure were implemented. The ambitions of municipal government continued unabated, and just as city leaders were beginning to feel very self-satisfied for having avoided a logjam of service demands requiring potentially massive tax increases, the seemingly bottomless well of revenue suddenly began to go dry.

The re-evaluation of responsibility for entire service areas under the New Federalism program is resulting in a shift to states and localities for the funding, the administration and the delivery of most social service programs. This process, which began with the tax and budget cuts of 1981, has escalated with the passage of the Gramm-Rudman Act.

Recently I was in Washington, and I was talking to Senator Gramm about this tax reform act, which can be very destructive to city governments. I can speak for Dallas and I can tell you that. Senator Gramm told a good joke on himself, and I seldom hear public officials tell good jokes on themselves. He was very pleased that they had issued a stamp with Gramm-Rudman on the face of the stamp. He said it wasn't very popular, but most important, it didn't stick. People were spitting on the wrong side.

But back to the problem I was discussing. Whereas in past years local municipalities might have turned to state government for help to fill the void, the downturn in energy revenue, as previously discussed, has effectively ruled out this option. So city governments in Texas find ourselves faced with the problem of assessing local service needs and finding the means to meet those needs.

We face an almost psychological quandary in this effort. How do we find ways of dealing with legitimate demands for public service without increasing property taxes, which may be really hard on homeowners and tenants alike, and without removing the low taxation incentive to economic development? As Professor Frantz said earlier, we are at a point now where we're really going to have to think.

As always, the first step in acknowledging the realities of a municipal situation is, what is the bottom line? And the bottom line for local government today is, if you want certain things done, do them and pay for them yourself, or they're not going to get done. The next step is a confrontation with existing and potential problems. This inevitably produces far more questions than answers, but we all know options for problem-solving begin to emerge or are eliminated with this initial probe.

Some of the questions my colleagues on the Dallas city council and I are asking include the following: What should the city do to meet the growing need for affordable, decent housing for middle, low, fixed and no-income people? How can city government help eliminate conditions leading to involuntary homelessness? To what extent should the city be involved in public-private efforts to provide emergency and short-term shelter? What can local entities do about the spiraling crime rate, the corresponding increase in the population of incarcerated individuals, the early parole of prisoners due to overcrowded facilities—persons who are not really ready for re-entry into society—and the effects of all this on our citizens? Which technologies and funding formulas are most appropriate in meeting the current and future mobility needs of residents? As Larry McMurtry said earlier today, urban gridlock does present a real threat to our cities. Are we as municipal leaders gaining maximum utilization of the talent, the expertise, and the resources available in the local community to meet policy challenges? Is the city providing sufficient assistance to business leaders in maintaining and improving our competitive edge in the regional, the national, and international markets? These are very challenging topics, and they represent the figurative nuts-and-bolts, bricks-and-mortar arena of the changing city government of our state in these rapidly changing times. We are thinking and we are working hard to find the right answers.

With all these issues facing us, the picture from municipal officials, while indeed sometimes bleak, is still one of optimism, because some of these problems can best be handled by the local government. For local government is a uniquely human-scale exercise, and it's a place where we can add humanism to a world of computerism. The equation for representative government on the community level is, even in this era of a faltering megalopolis, really rather basic. Most of us live in one city, rather than in another, by choice. There are certain aspects of life in that city which we enjoy, and certain other aspects of which we would like to see and experience much less. Whether we can satisfactorily articulate it or not, we all have in mind a design for the future of our city. When we go to vote on municipal election day, we vote for that candidate who comes closest to sharing our own local vision, or we vote against that candidate whose proposals and opinion most obviously conflict with our own. It is this human-scale exercise of local government, the human resource of opinion and insight, that is the greatest tool for the city official grappling with the new scope and the new character of municipal responsibility.

In city government we come together with our divergent points of view, and we attempt to construct policies which reflect the concerns of all our citizens. When a decision doesn't work, we have an opportunity on another day to amend that decision and to correct the flaws in our initial judgment. The American process of self-rule is rarely easy, but it almost always works, and works well.

In closing, let me say that I've gained quite a lot from this forum. I'm very grateful to the LBJ Library, the LBJ School of Public Affairs and *Texas Monthly* for bringing us all together. When I return to my desk in Dallas, the phone will ring and I will be asked all kinds of questions. People will want to have some help with a creek that has flooded. Or maybe they feel there's been an unfair zoning decision and they want to tell me about it before it comes to city council.

Or maybe somebody wants to discuss an unpaid ambulance bill. This is all very important, and I really do enjoy that job. But this kind of interaction with my colleagues today on other levels of government and professionals in other disciplines really does keep me aware of the whole picture and reinforces my perspective. It's going to help me do my job better, and I thank you for letting me be a part of it.

Paul Burka: When we were working at *Texas Monthly* on our sesquicentennial issue, a little refrain kept bouncing around in my head, an old cowboy song that I eventually mentioned in the magazine. There was an old refrain that the cowboys sang around the turn of the century; I will spare you my singing it, but I will recite it.

> I've got to leave old Texas now.
> For they have no use for the Longhorn cow;
> They've plowed and fenced my cattle range,
> And the people there are all so strange.

What's interesting about this is that people have been lamenting that Texas is changing for a hundred years, and more than that, I suppose, for a hundred and fifty years. The original three hundred settlers weren't so hot on the Tennesseeans and Kentuckians who followed.

We've seen a lot of changes in Texas politics in the last few years. Some of the victims, not all of whom, if any of whom, should we mourn, are brown paper bags, high school football coaches, Braniff, and conservative Democrats. People were saying that Texas wouldn't be the same after cattle, and now they're saying the same thing after oil. I've carefully constructed this talk to avoid talking about who's going to win the next governor's race, so I thought we might talk about sort of long-range trends and what we might look at in the way of change. What I think you will find is that the factors which have governed Texas public life for most of the twentieth century will probably continue to do so. There are at least four of those that we can identify. One is that Mike Kinsley, *The New Republic,* and "Let Them Rot in the Sun" notwithstanding, Texas is a poor state. It has been historically, so that in all of our history we never once reached the national average in personal per capita income until right at the very tail end of the oil boom, at which time we promptly slipped below it again, and are now dropping like a stone. That is not going to change. I think that there is very little prospect that we will arrive back at the national average any time soon.

The second factor is that we Texans do have a sense of destiny about us. We are a state that was once a nation, and Texans are very aware of that. That sense of destiny pervades Texas politics, but it also takes some rather perverse forms at times. We take pride sometimes in our isolationism, in our unsophistication, and in our anti-elitism. You can see it in education, and particularly in the way we fund higher education. I'll try to use an example where we won't gore anybody's ox right here. For an undergraduate student in English, Sul Ross gets the same amount of money as the University of Texas, which enables them to compete for faculty on exactly the same level. There is no attempt made to differentiate in higher education among universities.

So we have anti-elitism, unsophistication, and isolation which has taken some wonderful forms over the years. My favorite story in this regard is when Pa Ferguson became the first governor to take on the University of Texas and vetoed its appropriation back in the teens. When he was asked to explain it, he resorted to explaining, "Well, they're teaching foreign languages out there." When he got some strange looks he said, "Well, if English was good enough for Jesus, it's good enough for the school children of Texas."

I think that strain is still with us in more sophisticated guises these days. We still have a significant amount of xenophobia here, a colonial mentality. We want Yankee money, but we're not so sure that we want Yankees along with it. We're perfectly happy for Yankees to come invest here, but please, no Yankee bankers. You'll notice that the holding companies are desperately trying to keep the Yankees out. They now want to have banking over a twenty-state area, so that our broke banks can go out and buy broke banks in other states. There is this obsession that somehow we are prevented from realizing our destiny by control from elsewhere. You see that in oil right now. I did a story for the next issue of *Texas Monthly* about the New York Mercantile Exchange. I was struck time and again by oilmen I talked to who say that the reason the price of oil is going down is because of the speculators in New York. You heard exactly the same thing a hundred years ago from the cotton growers. The reason cotton was in trouble was that the New York speculators and railroads were doing it. So we still have that sense with us, and I don't think it is going to go away any time soon.

The fourth factor, growing out of the colonial mentality and the sense that we are an underdeveloped area, is the belief in good "bidness" as the guiding principle of Texas politics. In 1971 when I worked in the Senate, there were fifteen votes out of thirty-one senators for a corporate income tax. In 1984 in the House, there were thirteen votes out of a hundred and fifty House members for a corporate income tax. The "good bidness climate" has become sacred, and a consensus. You can see this fact in the rise of politicians like Henry Cisneros. When you think about the Mayor you have to realize that he is a member of a minority group that has been much discriminated against in Texas politics. That minority group is Aggies. Mayor Cisneros, like a good Aggie, is basically, I think, conservative in nature, and believes in government in partnership with business. In that respect, he is probably closer to another Aggie, Phil Gramm, than to many people in his own party. I do not think that this is very likely to change over the next years. If it does change and the Democrats nominate people like Lloyd Doggett, you won't hear very much about them after they get defeated.

What does all this mean? First of all, it means that the seventies were an aberration. They were a period during which we got rich, and we forgot where we came from. We've been reminded of it. I do not think you will see their like again. Even if oil comes back, twenty-five-dollar oil will not make a change, as distinguished Professor Weinstein pointed out. Not because it won't make a difference, but because we have learned now not to buy onto the myth of fifty-dollar oil. The oil world is different in any event. You will not see the booms and busts. You may see a steady growth in the industry, but you won't see the boom mentality again. The New York bankers will not let it happen, and they'll be in control by then.

Second, the unique folk culture that we have is much stronger than people who worry about Texas think. I think it will survive. We may not be able to bring brown bags into restaurants anymore, but we still buy trucks at a rate four times the national average. So there is still this unique culture in Texas, and I think that will continue.

Third, whatever changes do take place in Texas, and they will continue to be substantial, will take place largely outside the political process, as they largely have in the past, and that can't be all bad.

I would like to address a question to a couple of my colleagues on the extremes of the table here. I believe, Mr. Weinstein, you said we have had economic growth, but not economic development, implying that we need that. Jim, you were talking about the farm's future. But what about the essential problem: to have economic development, you've got to have resources, and what do we have to sell, if we are competing with other places? And, Jim, in terms of agriculture's future, it's fine to talk about this stuff, but we don't have any water. Again, it's the resource problem. What is the future for the Panhandle? Is there any future for it, or are they just going to be dry-land farmers?

Jim Hightower: Number one, we do have water. We have water that can be used a lot more efficiently than it now is being used.

Paul Burka: Don't tell me you've got religion. You want to pump it out from East Texas?

Jim Hightower: No, nonsense. We have water in West Texas right now, including water in cities—that is slurry water, which is a waste product—that could be used in agriculture. Other countries are doing very well with that. We have salt water all over West Texas that we could use for production of certain crops. It is a natural resource that we consider a waste product now, but other countries make use of it.

That is not to say that we should continue to produce just water-wasting crops out there, but it doesn't mean there is no agricultural future. You shift to crops that are more efficient users of water, you shift to dry-land techniques of agricultural production, and you shift to conservation systems that make sense. We had a proposal out of the Texas Senate last year for an agricultural water conservation plan that would have saved 20 per cent of the water that agriculture uses. More water would have been saved than if you outlawed indoor plumbing in the state of Texas. It made so much sense that the House of Representatives water resource committee rejected it out of hand, and it didn't get out of committee. But we did get a little proposal out of there that I think will show the efficacy of a proposal like that, that indeed you can save substantial amounts of water in agriculture, so that we can go back to the legislature next session to get the Senate version of the bill or something like that put back in.

Bernard Weinstein: That's a very good question. Your question was, what do we sell? Traditionally we've sold agricultural products, we've sold energy products. Today we are a big seller of defense goods. Tourism is a fairly big industry in this state. Any regional economy exists on what it produces, what it has to offer to other people in other regions. Now, agriculture and energy are not going away. They will continue to be major sectors of the Texas economy, and we should not turn our backs on them. We want to keep them as healthy and as viable as we can, because that is where our comparative advantages lie at the present time. The defense thing is propping up places like Dallas-Fort Worth, Austin-San Antonio, but we all know that defense spending is cyclical. It has probably peaked and won't be generating the jobs three or four years from now that it is today.

But the real challenge is to find new things to sell. As I said before, I don't know what those products are going to be, but we are not going to get there unless we continue to make the kinds of investments that we have just started to make in education and other aspects of human capital.

Let me make one quick point. Jim and Earl and you, Paul, have all been talking about myths, some myths that maybe we need to dispel. I'd like to add one to the list. That is the "bidness climate" myth that the way to encourage business growth in this state is to keep taxes low and unions out. That just doesn't play anymore. That is probably totally irrelevant. There is a role for government to play in economic development. There are certain kinds of state and local government spending that have a very heavy impact on economic development, and we shouldn't forget that. The state of Colorado is going through some of the same problems that we are here in Texas with declining revenues. The initial political reaction has been, "Let's tighten our belt, but let's not increase taxes." The Colorado Chamber of Commerce passed a resolution, presented it to the legislature, and said, "Don't do that. We are willing to pay higher taxes in order to maintain services, and in particular to continue making this commitment to education that we've started in this state." There is an interesting lesson there that we maybe ought to consider in Texas.

Paul Burka: I think you are half right in the sense that taxes are a myth. But the last person I talked to about unions, Buddy Temple, who's on the board of Temple Inland, says that they do look at labor. So whether you are pro-union or not, they do look at that.

Bernard Weinstein: It is not a question of being pro-union or anti-union. It's just that the union thing is very, very irrelevant today because number one, corporate relocations and business expansions—people coming from out of state and setting up facilities—just doesn't happen very much. Second, if you look at the industries that are growing in Texas and around the country, they are not unionized industries, they are outside of that traditional blue-collar sector.

Dave McNeely: I am afraid that we have run out of time. I've come out of this with the idea that fifty years from now my great-granddaughter should be a compassionate small-family farmer with a computer. She will send her kids to school at a very early age. She will believe in state and city rights, but also accept responsibilities, and she will not fear unions or an income tax.

GENERAL DISCUSSION

William Broyles, Jr.: I am reminded of the man who took a speed reading course, and the first book he read was *War and Peace.* He told his friend that he had just finished *War and Peace* and said, "I read it in fifteen minutes." His friend said, "You read *War and Peace* in fifteen minutes?" He said, "Yes, it's about Russia." For the last few hours, I think we have had so much good material, so many insights, that it is not immediately clear what all of this has been about. Before we begin to get into this I want to make just a couple of personal points and observations. I have just returned to Texas after spending six years in California and New York. I confess this at the beginning. I have sinned, but I have learned the error of my ways, and I hope that I will be welcomed back into the fold. One reason I wanted to come back was to be part of this sesqui—however Mark White says it—this great celebration. But it turns out that it's been a little bittersweet. As Professor Weinstein has pointed out, instead of these wonderful articles in the national press about all that we have achieved, we have been reading about Texas being in trouble: "Let Them Rot in the Sun;" "Cap an Oil Well, Starve a Texan." It may be news to us, but not everyone out there likes us.

There has been a certain patina of glee in all of these reports. "We had it coming" is the underlying theme. We Texans have been too cocky, too loud, too rich. We are the blue-eyed Arabs reaping the benefits of an energy-starved nation's sufferings. As Paul Burka has pointed out, this particular myth is cruelly false. We are, in fact, a poor state. Houston has more poor people than are in the entire city of Newark, New Jersey. Texas has more poor people than the state of New York. In Houston, where I have brilliantly picked to settle, people say that we have recently contracted an epidemic of RAIDS, that is Recently Acquired Income Deficiency Syndrome. And we don't like it, because we've always believed that if we get up early, work hard, work longer than anyone else, we will do well. But we are now confronting a time in which no matter how early we get up and how hard we work we may not do well. It is that testing of the myth that Larry McMurtry talked about: that we are an optimistic state; that things will always get better. As he, Mayor Cisneros, Professor Weinstein, and others stressed, there is no guarantee of this.

We have always had that frontier faith in taming nature and reaping its riches. My best example of this came from Bob Kleberg, the ongoing genius of the King Ranch. He took the King Ranch into Australia, and he was asked what's the difference between the Australian frontier and the Texas frontier. He said this: "In Texas, we built the railroads and the roads first, and we just assumed that people and commerce would fill them. In Australia, they waited for the people and commerce before building the railroads and roads out into the outback. There are no roads and railroads there yet."

That faith has really been tested. We have been built and based upon growth, bigger, better, more. Even as Mayor Cisneros ticked off his tour of Texas, and all of the problems in the different regions, particularly with everything rooted in the old culture, oil, agriculture, Mexico, he went on to say that we would have twenty million people by the turn of the century. Why? Isn't that a statistic, no different than our talking about eighty-five-dollar oil in 1985? Bernard Weinstein says we won't grow, that it will be more like the sixties. A statistic which has stuck in my mind about the sixties is that during the entire decade of the sixties, fewer people moved into Texas from other states than moved into Connecticut from other states. As Paul Burka said, perhaps the seventies have been an aberration. After all, Pennsylvania, Michigan, and New York aren't gaining population, why should we?

One question that I think we should be addressing here is, if we don't gain population, what does that mean? And if we do, how do we make it happen? How we can be, as the Mayor said, "masters of our destiny"?

One area that I also wanted to talk about early is education. Having been gone for six years, if I were going to pick the single biggest change in Texas right now, it would be in the attitude toward education. When I left, certain members of the board of regents whose pictures hang in the LBJ Library were talking about having a university the football team could be proud of. I don't hear much of that now. In fact, if we look at the no-pass, no-play legislation, we can see something which in its essence goes to the heart of what many of us were talking about, which is that our traditions are what make us who we are, but that they also can get in our way. Here is a case in which I think we have taken the nettle of the tradition of football being what high school is all about, and turned it on its head, and said that high school is for learning. That's the sort of thing, as we're talking about improved education and so on, that seems to me a concrete step. Basically, we say we want education.

The other thing I want to say is this, and this is not good news. I have done a lot of traveling in the last six years, and everywhere I have gone—Ohio, Israel, Germany, California, New Mexico, Colorado, New England—the following things are said: "We have to diversify out of our traditional economy. We have to focus on human resources and our people. We have to improve education and we have to grasp the high tech frontier." I haven't heard a thing different today than

I've heard in ten different places I've been. The question is, how do *we* make it happen?

There are many more we can cover. Are we going to keep growing or not? Are we going to be managing a stable population and economy, or are we going to try to have a growing one? Since education was so focused upon during these discussions, it is fine to have that as a goal. Talk is cheap. What do we do about it?

Felicia Jeter: My name is Felicia Jeter of KHOU-TV in Houston. I am a Texan by choice. I am from Atlanta. I've lived in Los Angeles, New York, and Chicago. I am real concerned, now, about all of the things we have been talking about here today. If you want to get my attention, since I am from Houston now, use three words: diversification, jobs, and the third would, of course, be ratings, but that's another conference.

I am very concerned when we get together like this and I don't hear enough specifics. That scares me to death, because I hear us saying, generally, yes, we have to diversify, but I don't hear us being specific enough, and talking about enough breakdowns of the areas, things that we can do that spread us out from those two legs on that two-legged stool. I am real concerned, too, about how we get to the future from this present. It is good for us to talk about the necessity of planning. I am concerned that the need for planning goes against the grain of the Texas spirit somehow, and maybe that's how we got here from there. I am real concerned that we have so many people who are out of work, and we are talking about the importance of education as a part of our future. What are we going to do with all these people and our present problems? How is that going to impact on whether or not our future is going to be positive and healthy? I need some answers.

Roland Boyd: My name is Roland Boyd. I'm a lawyer in McKinney, Texas. First, I would like to comment on the six lady panelists. I'm convinced after listening to them that when women quit darning socks and learned how to read, we men have been losing ground ever since.

Let's get specific. I think it's all a question of priorities. There are four things that are essential to the quality of life and humanity. Of those four, in my judgment, the only ones that have been mentioned are first, energy, raw energy; second, mobility. I think that those are the bottom two of the four. The first is drinking water development; the second is food. Of course, we need energy and mobility, but if you want economic growth, you develop the water resources of this state. You will have population growth, you will have economic development, and people will go back to work. We're proving that on the East Fork of the Trinity in North Texas. Eleven little cities in 1951, when the North Texas Water District was created, had a total combined population of 33,000. Those eleven little cities now have about a quarter of a million people. That is just one example of what will happen. You talk about rate of return? Yes, Austin, if you want a rate of return, you put it in water resource development, and then in salvaging arable land, and then in making the people mobile, then in creating the energy. And it will all fall in place.

Felix D. Almaraz, Jr.: My name is Felix Almaraz; I am from San Antonio. First, I was not responsible for the Mayor's historical errors, because he went to A&M and didn't take my course. But a word about my Mayor and all this stress that he places on technology. It seems to me that we're not questioning all this high tech; we're accepting it as a cult. What concerns me is that students come to me, questioning my prerogative of assigning to them books to read. They say, "Why should we read books when we just have to write scientific reports?" The problem seems to me that we are falling behind on plain basic English communication skills. That concerns me. Only one panelist addressed the need for the humanities. A lot of emphasis was placed on other areas.

In terms of the quality of municipal services, why is it that our civic leaders tell us about an energy crisis and then continue putting up more traffic lights? Why don't they question that? I would like to see somebody run for public office on a platform saying they are for fewer traffic lights, so as to move the people rather than stopping them. And what about the quality of work in municipal government? It seems that there's so much stress on gadgetry. Secretaries can't function if the typewriter goes out or if the computer goes out. They cannot communicate with you. They cannot give you basic information, because they've learned to become dependent upon the computer.

I'm concerned about educational reform. We've heard so much about House Bill 72. Everyone who is familiar with government knows that a governor simply proposes and the legislature disposes. The Governor seems to be catching all the flak for this House Bill 72, but it was the legislature that enacted it. Yet the teachers are out there talking about all this burden of paperwork that has now become their responsibility on account of House Bill 72. If they are required to do this, then where are they going to find the time for quality education? Those are my concerns. Thank you, sir.

William Broyles, Jr.: I would like to focus for a moment on the sources of our economy and its future, water being one, often called a more important liquid to Texas than oil. I would like someone also to pick up on Professor Weinstein's statement that the oil card has been played, that it doesn't matter if oil goes back to twenty-five dollars again. I would be curious if anyone has reactions to Jim Hightower's wonderful world of new agriculture. Let's talk about these sources of the economy.

The other thing I've noticed which is odd to me, having been in Houston, is that no one today has mentioned space at all, and I'm just curious as to what role that might play.

Howard T. Odum: I'm H. T. Odum from the University of Florida, a visiting professor here with the LBJ School for this year.

Texans are in the process of doing some cutting back for the first time since 1933. But fifteen-dollar oil gives you about nine-to-one more stimulus to the economy, and this acts on 80 per cent of the Texas economy. So you're going to have more stimulus to the economy than you are loss, due to this temporary drop in oil. The real trouble comes when the oil price goes back up in the world as a whole and other resources get deeper and deeper and harder to get and more expensive. Then Texas, along with the rest of the country, is forced to level its growth and to come down. The exercise of considering some adjustments to coming down is a good thing for Texas to do now, because the real marathon is coming up four, five, six years from now. Now, how do you come down and is that bad? As a culture that's used to thinking that up is good, Texans have got to learn to think that coming down is good.

William Broyles, Jr.: That's going to be the trick. You're making it real hard for them.

Howard T. Odum: No, no, it's easier than you think. We're trying to start a center at our university in Florida to learn how to do this. Maybe we need to have one here as a companion. I'll give you specific examples. These apply to the present government. The proper way to come back is to ask everybody to cut their salary 10 per cent. When you do that, then you're democratic; everybody can decide what is their luxury. And you don't increase crime and you don't increase welfare and costs. So that's the obvious way to come down instead of firing a few people or dropping programs. But it's a new idea. Things that you do going up are not the ones you do coming down. Another example is the problem with agriculture. It has been "Let's increase production." Now, it's "Let's cut costs even if we have to lower production." So that means that you can cut back on your machinery and chemicals and that you put your unemployed urban Houston young people to work back on the farms for the first time.

William Broyles, Jr.: Sounds like Cambodia to me. It didn't work there either.

Howard T. Odum: You see, you see, that's a mindset: "This guy must be a nut."

Let me give you two more examples. On the way up, borrowing is an advantage. It's like discounting and so on. On the way down, it is not. The whole set of business banking behavior is different.

The fourth and last one is the extra steel running up and down in those four extra trucks that we heard about in U.S. highways, particularly Texas. Cutting back on that waste of running steel around in circles is enough to make Texas products perhaps 5 or 10 per cent more competitive when the savings are spread back through the economy.

These are details and mechanisms of how you come down and how you plan to come down and how you help people see it. They are going to stumble into this the hard way, but can we learn to regard progress as down? Anything that works people learn to adapt to. Within a generation, they'll be teaching that that's what's right and that the last generation was nutty for doing it some other way. Your children are going to say that you were blind, that you couldn't see that the proper promised land for the next period of time is not up, and that cutting back and learning to regulate the population to keep the resource per person constant is our new mission. Part of this school ought to dedicate itself to this; some part of the government ought to dedicate itself to this.

William Broyles, Jr.: It is certainly true, particularly true in areas of Houston, that those users of petroleum products, the petrochemical industry being the most obvious one, have an opportunity to grow and do better now. Of course, they are competing around the world with lower-cost industries that are doing the same thing.

Roger M. Olien: I'm Roger Olien, University of Texas, Permian Basin. I remember a book that came out about fifteen years ago—most of you have read it—called *The Last Boom,* by Clark and Helbooty. Curiously, it preceded the most recent boom by just a few years, and yet it had that title. That reflects the historic unpredictability of energy economics. Rather than take up the notion that we've played the last card, we ought to assume that there were thirteen in the suit to begin with, that we have not played the last card at all. Perhaps we've exhausted the face cards in the deck, but the industry has a long if unpredictable future. Unpredictability is above all what we have to keep in mind. Many of you know that the oil industry is in trouble today because, among other reasons, our record at forecasting energy economics has been deplorable. We've had very little experience at it. I'm suggesting that we shouldn't order the pallbearers and make arrangements soon. We ought to maintain a healthy skepticism about any kind of projection.

If we look at the industry's history in this state and the consequences of the last boom, we see one thread running through the whole story: that those plans and decisions that were made by businessmen or regulatory bodies have been made in Texas and in the rest of the country with scant regard for the social consequences of those decisions. We have to learn from that and try as best we can to avoid doing the same thing as Texas enters a post-industrial age.

Harold M. Hyman: Rice University. I'm a historian, and I firmly believe in the relevant dictum of the poet W. H. Auden, "Never sit next to a statistician nor commit a social science." On the other hand, I know that many of my colleagues in history never agree on the use of history for present social problems. We're pathologists, not futurologists. And so I've listened with great interest and attention and disbelief and skepticism to much of what went on, especially this afternoon, but in part also this morning. My incredulity arose from the historical role assigned to the growth of a two-party structure in the state, which seems to me to be different from any other two-party structure in any other state. In the latter, they tend toward the center and they tend to attract voters from wide spectra of class interests, et cetera, into the mainstream parties. This does not seem to be the development of the growth of the second major party in Texas, at least to the present. I hope it becomes healthier.

Second, I certainly would not be as confident as some speakers today about the allegedly positive role of Texas entrepreneurs in accelerating beneficent and widespread distributive social and economic change. To be sure, historical scholars at least have not paid much attention to entrepreneurs in American history. We've paid much more attention to slave owners, to slaves and to other kinds of people at the extremes. But there is good scholarship growing on the center, and it's that scholarship that makes me very, very skeptical indeed about the happy role which has been assumed, at least, and alleged during much of the proceedings today. The hymns to deregulation make me worry about the Darwinian jungle out of which regulations grew.

Karen Mosman: My name is Karen Mosman. I'm with the Sesquicentennial Commission. At the risk of being charged with believing our own propaganda, it has been my observation that it is tourism that is the second industry in Texas, recently arrived. Yet at this forum I have heard that word only one time. I'm wondering why. One option might be that it plugs into the Texas mystique, and the rubophobia that was mentioned comes into play. We maybe don't want those people gawking at us. Or is it our myopic two-legged stool has always been oil and cattle? Can we not see this other industry? Do we not know how to develop it? It's an observation. This is missing from this forum, and I'm wondering why.

Neal Spelce: My name is Neal Spelce, Neal Spelce Communications, and you hit a tremendously good point that relates to what Felicia was saying. Let me give just a few quick statistics. The state of Texas was thriving and rolling in the early sixties. For oil and gas and agriculture, momentum was going well. Today those are in a decline, amorphous, just sitting out there. And today, tourism, in terms of revenue generated, is at least number three and, by some counts, number two, ahead of agriculture. In the early sixties the state of Texas ranked twenty-sixth in the nation in tourist revenue. Today we rank third in the nation behind only California and Florida and ahead of New York State itself. The emphasis is there, the momentum is there.

Another statistic: in 1985, hotel-motel bed tax, revenues that go to the State of Texas General Revenue Fund, were up 40 per cent from 1984. So far this year the revenue from the bed tax is up another 20 to 30 per cent, increasing momentum to a fulfillment of the economy in this state.

Here is strong impetus; the momentum is going the right way. We don't have to spend money to educate the children of tourists who come to Texas. We don't have to spend money to give them fire protection in our own communities. Yet they are coming here, spending dollars, providing jobs for us, and then they go back home leaving those dollars behind and helping our economy. There is no single area of this state of Texas, no matter where it's located, that cannot and should not benefit directly from tourism's impact. The major attraction of this state as a tourist destination is its diversity. And that diversity of course is present throughout every area geographically around this state of Texas. You hit a good point and one that has been overlooked and should not have been overlooked.

Alex Burton: I'm Alex Burton with KRLD in Dallas, and you're absolutely right. I'll give you some stats now.

There has been no mention of the hospitality industry, and it is unquestionably the second largest industry in the state today. This year it will generate sixteen billion dollars. Agriculture will generate ten billion dollars, and a goodly portion of that ten billion dollars will be support payments from the federal government. So far what we have seen here today has been a paean to the oil industry. What I say is that if there is diversity here in the state, it is through the hospitality industry.

The problem comes in generating the capital necessary to promote tourism. State government cut its advertising budget by half a million bucks. If you don't advertise, nobody knows you're there. That's poor business, in spite of the arguments we got that the legislature was "pro-bidness." I don't think it is.

No mention has been made at all of small business. That's where jobs come from: small business. Not from gigantic businesses that move here to build Saturn cars. By the year 2000 more than 50 per cent of the new jobs that will be created in the state will come from small businesses of fewer than twenty people. No mention of that was made at all.

Oscar J. Martinez: My name is Oscar Martinez. I'm from the University of Texas at El Paso.

I have a comment about education because I think it's very important at this critical stage that we find ourselves in. But I want to preface it with a comment about feelings that you find in certain parts of Texas, and El Paso is one of these places. As a historian, I'm interested in the events of 1836 and the sentiments in Texas at that time, when people were complaining about the treatment that they got from the central government in Texas. They complained that they were neglected, that they didn't have enough autonomy, that they were not getting a fair deal. Well, in fact there are places in Texas where that feeling is still alive. El Paso is one of these places. El Paso is far away from the center of power, from the center of the economy and the demographic center of the state. A lot of people don't know much about El Paso, but we have a city of half a million people with another city across the border, Ciudad Juarez, that has more than a million people. We share many common characteristics with other communities along the border. There is a certain culture from Brownsville all the way to El Paso. One of the problems these areas have shared historically is neglect by the state. We heard some things from some panelists about the poverty there and the desperate economic conditions.

We have an opportunity to do something about these problems in education that are directly related to economic development and poor conditions that you find in places like El Paso. Public Law 72 was great for the state, and the poor population benefited a great deal from that. Now that we have a select committee looking at higher education, we have another opportunity to do something fairly important. If you look at the way resources are distributed in higher education, you find a tremendous disparity and a lot of discrimination against institutions that don't have the political power base. Higher education in the state of Texas is highly politicized, and this has hurt various parts of Texas and the Texas border with Mexico in particular. There are some members of the Select Committee on Higher Education here, and I hope that this condition will be taken seriously, so that resources for higher education are more fairly distributed, so that universities that are based in El Paso, Harlingen and other places that have underdeveloped universities get a chance to improve their situation, and so that the lack of access to educational opportunity that the border people now suffer from is corrected. The formula that the state legislature uses to distribute money is heavily weighted in favor of certain institutions in the state. There are only two institutions that have access to the available fund that comes out of the Permanent University Fund, and those are the University of Texas at Austin and Texas A&M. The University of Texas at El Paso and other universities have no access to that fund, and as a result they have very few programs that are available to the poor population.

Let me finish. I came a long way to attend this conference. I left another one that I was partly responsible for organizing, and I want to finish my points, if you will permit me. We're at a crossroads here; there is a committee looking at this. I'm hopeful that these disparities are taken seriously. It's a specific issue; there's an opportunity to really bring Texas into the twentieth century.

I'm from El Paso and I graduated from high school. I didn't come to the University of Texas at Austin or any other institution in the state, because there really wasn't interest in recruiting students from the border and in giving them opportunities. I went to California and got all my education in California. I got a chance to see how the California system works. That state distributes resources in a more equitable manner. UCLA, Berkeley, the University of California at San Diego, I was at these various institutions, and things work a lot better there. Mayor Cisneros made reference to the fact that California is way ahead of us, and they certainly are. We have an opportunity here to do something very specific, to improve the situation of our population and stimulate economic development through advanced education. But we have to eliminate this discrimination that currently exists that is hurting the border population, predominantly Hispanic, at the present time.

Wilhelmina Delco: We on the select committee, and I happen to be a member of the select committee, not only went to El Paso but we went to three other areas that are specifically identified with either the border or the Hispanic population. So I think that the select committee is very well aware of the concerns of that area. But I'd also like to correct a question. I was the author of Proposition 2, which expanded the Permanent University Fund to include all of the facilities of the University of Texas, one of which is the University of Texas at El Paso, so that they could benefit from that fund in five areas. Previously the Permanent University Fund only talked about construction, and everything that was not spent on bonding construction was reserved for the University of Texas at Austin and A&M at College Station for academic excellence. Now that fund, thanks to the voters of Texas by a 75 per cent approval vote, is expanded to include not only new construction but major repair and rehabilitation, capital improvement like labs and computers and things like that, library acquisitions and major new land acquisitions, so that there is a broad base of availability for the Permanent Fund. And since we have seventeen colleges outside of the UT-A&M system, a new fund was constitutionally created to address those institutions for the same five areas. It appropriates a hundred million dollars, top draw on general revenue.

But I want to address something else; I just wanted to respond to that. The thing I wanted to address was the whole question of education, and I, too, would like to throw out a couple of statistics. Mayor Cisneros is exactly right. The fastest growing new population in Texas is black and brown. The people who will go to college and high school are already born, so we're not making up figures. We're talking about people who are already on earth. So the question becomes very significant as to how we define education and what we talk about when we say availability of education. Those are questions of access and quality. Are we saying that we want to make sure our universities become those of the first class? As Meg Wilson stated, only one major department in one university has national or international recognition. I submit that quality is as quality does. If we're talking about a population of the future, it may be more important to make sure a lot of our people read and write than it is to anoint a few people in a few institutions that we hope at some point will produce the miracle of economic development.

Another aspect that we ought to look at is, outside of that fast growing minority population, the largest growing population in this country is people over eighty. And therein lies a great deal of contradiction, because as one population grows older, it is going to resist the proposals that we make to help this newly emerging population. So we're going to see more people resisting bond elections and tax elections that talk about public schools and public services where they don't identify directing those services to older people. I think we've got to deal with that in Texas.

On the select committee we're divided into three committees that are very important. One is access and quality, trying to say: are we better off looking at open admissions on all levels? Or are we better off with the so-called assessment vehicles like testing: testing people in, testing people along the way and testing people out, and basing credentials on tests? That's a question that we must address and we must answer in Texas, particularly since there are significant elements of the population that flat-out don't test well. That's one question.

The second question that the select committee is looking at is funding governance and management. There's a whole lot of talk about the fat in higher education, and it's interesting to note that when we talked about reforming public education, everybody went in with the idea that we were going to have to raise more money because we were going to have to pay people better if we wanted them to do a better job. In higher education, everybody is saying the best way to deal with increasing the quality of higher education is "cutting out the fat." That is to say, cutting money out, not putting money in. I submit that that's not going to work. We are in a competitive economy. Just as we attracted all these great people to Texas, we are going to lose them if we don't give them better salaries in a lot of instances. There's not that much fat.

The third thing that we're looking at is a whole question of funding from the standpoint of merger. Do we have superfluous institutions? Should we, in the name of providing good educational quality, close down some schools, or close down some kinds of education? We ought to be very serious about that. It's very easy to say we've got too many schools. But if the object is to educate people from where they are to where we want them to be, we'd better look at the fact that a lot of our people are undereducated and simply cannot or will not go to UT Austin for that education. So a lot of our institutions are serving very important purposes.

When we talk about higher education, we unfailingly talk as if the movement is from high school to senior-level institutions. We've left out completely in this discussion the whole aspect of community colleges. Community colleges in Texas educate 60 per cent of the freshmen and sophomores, a third of the minorities, and have the largest single adult population in this state. They're within fifty miles of every community. As we look at a future where people will be changing jobs three to six times in their work lifetime, they will turn to community colleges for their continuing education. So we can't talk about education as if it's either kindergarten through twelfth grade or UT-level education. We need to talk about education on the continuing spectrum.

The other aspect that the select committee is looking at is research and economic development. It's great to talk about research, but we define research as high-tech gimmickry and gadgetry. There's a whole lot of research that needs to be done and looked at: how people learn, how people grow, how people work, how people live. If we're talking about a world that's getting smaller, we've got to do more than play Rambo. We'd better look at trying to live with people. That's a legitimate function of higher education and all education in this country. If we're going to have any future at all, it has to be thoroughly grounded in education. In Texas we're going to get what we pay for, and we're not overtaxed, in my opinion. If we're not willing to pay now, we're going to pay later. Along with our education population, our prison population is moving right along, too.

William Broyles, Jr.: Since the California system has been held up to us, how do they do it better than we do, if they do? My memory of it is that it is a system of interlocking colleges and universities, each with different functions, roles, funding, and admission requirements.

Raymond E. Frisbie: I'm Ray Frisbie, from the other university, Texas A&M, and a graduate of the University of California. Let me address your first point, and then I'd like to make a point that follows up on the lady's comment on research and demonstration or extension.

The University of California system essentially is nine universities. There's also the University of California state college system, which is another set of universities. They're all funded, as I understand it, through a state appropriation that is formularized and distributed throughout the state. Taxes in California are naturally higher, depending on who is governor and the sentiment of the legislature at the time. They can go up and down. Texas universities have increased faculty salaries significantly to attract fine people to the University of Texas, Texas A&M and others of the fine university system. We don't yet have the heritage of the University of California at Berkeley, UCLA, San Diego, Santa Barbara, Riverside and so forth, which years ago invested heavily in higher education. They're seeing a growth and an accruement of that investment. It's paying substantial dividends at this time.

On a one-to-one basis, if you just look at the money part of it, we're highly competitive. We're missing major factors in support personnel, in facilities, and things to go along with bringing talented people into the Texas university system. Coming out of the University of California system, I took it for granted that the facilities would be there, that the support staff would be there, and that they'd be well paid. These elements are important so that we as professors don't have to spend time worrying about typing, lab technicians, and doing the other things. We want to do the things that we're basically hired to do. Those are the major factors.

I'd like to comment a little bit on research. Being a representative of the Texas Agricultural Experiment Station and Extension Service, and also having some interest in the Water Resources Institute at Texas A&M, I think we're in a position in higher education to begin to recruit some very talented students. My dilemma as a university professor is how you recruit people from the black and brown population of this state into my special area, which happens to be agriculture. Most of our brown students come from Latin America. In the Department of Entomology, we do not have a black undergraduate, and this really concerns me. We have the opportunity in agriculture; it's the other leg of the stool. We're in a time of very dynamic and constant change. The major commodities that we're dealing with are very high-value crops. So there's a business incentive; there's a technical-scientific incentive; there's an agricultural policy incentive. We can present the whole gamut, and what we're struggling with now is how can we recruit these people into this part of education?

Ricardo Romo: I'd like to add to that. I'm a native Texan, UT graduate, University of California graduate, and I had occasion to teach at Berkeley last year. My name is Ricardo Romo; I'm from the History Department here at UT Austin. The University of California system was launched in the 1880s, in the aftermath of the gold strike. California had a head start over Texas and other parts of the country with the gold money. It built the railroads and a system superior to ours. It built harbors and built a university system.

When I attended the University of California in 1970, UC Irvine had just been built. Today it's twenty-fifth in the nation as one of the top schools. California doesn't have a flagship university like many states. It has numerous campuses that are considered flagship universities.

It also has a very good community college system that we don't seem to have here. There are reasons for success: the concentration of population really helps California, while in Texas we have to educate a population that is spread and dispersed. At Berkeley last year, 50 per cent of the freshman class was people of color: Asian, black, and Hispanic. Half of the new law school class was, also. They're doing something to address this issue of educating the population that is going to be the majority population in that state by the year 2000.

Gregory Curtis: I'm Greg Curtis of *Texas Monthly*. When we talk about education, although amount of money of course is a tremendous problem, an equal problem is the allocation of that money. As I listened to the panel today, the goals for education in Texas were two: one, that education would help us meet the challenge in terms of science and industry, and then second, and more important, that education would help expand the frontier of the spirit and of the intellect.

And as I walk around the campus of the University of Texas, what concerns me is that I see so many things that are applicable to neither of those goals. Schools are devoted to fields of endeavor that, however worthy they may or may not be, really have nothing to do with science or art or the spirit. And tremendous amounts of money are going into them. Tremendous numbers of students are studying in them. To me, it is a tremendous burden on the whole university. I think that the university budget, though I would support any increase in its size, could be better spent. Many of the people on the panel talked about rethinking the things that have brought us here, about casting aside old myths and old treasured aspects of Texas. Our concept of a state university should be one of those things. We should take a very good and hard look at what is currently offered at the University of Texas. How much does it cost and can we afford it anymore, in light of the challenges that we need to prepare the people of Texas to face?

Cathy Mincberg: My name is Cathy Mincberg, and I am vice president of the school board in Houston, Texas. I'd like to comment from a little different perspective, and that is one of public education, secondary and elementary education. Most of the conversation I've heard this morning reflects on higher education, and while I'm a great believer in that, having several degrees, I'm going to put the emphasis for right now on students in grades kindergarten through twelve, and on pre-kindergarten.

I'm a former teacher, and as any good teacher would do, I would like to applaud you and give you a little encouragement in other areas. I'd like to applaud you for focusing today, even if not by design, on the fact that development of human resources is going to make a difference. The encouragement I'm going to give you is that we have faced and have gone through a very traumatic time, and that is reform of education in the state of Texas. It has been extremely costly in terms of agony, money, political lives, people's anxieties. But we don't see the leadership in this room standing up and saying, "We support the kinds of changes that have occurred." I'm not sure you're aware of most of them, because we tend to focus on no pass-no play, which I support as a great change. I don't know if you can imagine what life was like before House Bill 72. To be a young, brand-new or even a veteran teacher, to be locked in a room seven hours a day with thirty-five six-year-olds and no time to go to the bathroom was an incredible experience.

William Broyles, Jr.: For them or for you?

Cathy Mincberg: Probably both.

We have received the kind of product that we've put in the effort for. We have kids who go to college and have to take remedial courses for two years. We have to pay for that, because they leave public education institutions in pitiful shape. We need you to go out there now and support local politicians, who are under terrible pressures, and to raise money to support the reforms of House Bill 72. It is costing us a fortune to lower the class size in kindergarten and first and second grade. It is costing us a fortune to provide the classrooms. As a matter of fact, the school districts in the Valley just don't have the buildings and they can't afford to pay for them. There we've redistributed the money, a little away from the rich and a little to the poor, not completely equitable but a good attempt, and no one is out there saying, "Good job. Well done, we support that. We live in an affluent area, and we understand. We're going to have to raise taxes to support a quality program in other areas of the state."

I don't know if you quite understand the diversity out there, but we have school districts that have a million dollars' worth of property value per child to support that child in education. We have other districts as low as twenty thousand dollars in value of property tax to support the education of a child. So consequently we have enormous disparities. House Bill 72, while flawed, and I will have to admit that, is full of enormous progress. But nobody is out there saying anything good about it. We are probably going to defeat a governor based on his stance to take a tough decision and support those reforms. We are probably going to defeat lots of legislators because they were tough, and lots of local school board officials because they don't know what to do now. They've got a mandate from the state, and they're going to have to raise local property taxes to meet that. So unless the leadership in this room and around the state comes out in a very loud voice, we are going to lose enormous ground, ground that has brought us into the correct century and that we need to continue.

Oscar J. Martinez: I just wanted to add a point to illustrate what I was talking about. People who live along the border who want to get a graduate education are prevented from having access to those programs because they simply don't exist along the border. The programs are concentrated in other universities. We have a couple of super-universities in the state, and some of the others are pretty good and have advanced programs. But then there are all the others which are prevented, because of a Coordinating Board policy, from having advanced programs.

How many Ph.D. programs do you find in border institutions? How many medical schools, how many law schools, how many other advanced graduate programs do you find there? Where does a student from El Paso go if, for family or economic reasons, he or she cannot attend UT Austin, or the University of Houston, or even Texas Tech? What does a place-bound professional do, who would like to go beyond the master's degree? And we need these people in El Paso. What do they do?

A Coordinating Board rule says that El Paso is to have only one doctoral program. We've got to eliminate that. That's what I'm talking about. We've got to help Pan American University; we've got to help other universities in the state.

We've got to get away from overconcentrating programs and resources in certain universities. UT Austin has nine hundred-plus endowed professorships. The University of Texas at El Paso has two or three, each worth a hundred thousand dollars. I understand that the University of Texas at San Antonio has two. That's what I'm talking about. We believe in a flagship university at UT Austin; we're proud of it as Texans, but the disparity is just unacceptable. We've got to do something about that.

Lyn Dunsavage: My name is Lyn Dunsavage; I'm with the *Dallas Downtown News*. Two things: something that has bothered me today is that we have not talked about the development of two classes of people in the state that are going to have an enormous impact in the near future, and certainly by the year 2000. One that has been alluded to by Miss Delco is the aged population. When we have an enormous growth in people that are over sixty years of age, and we will have a blossoming of that particular sector of the population by the year 2000, that is going to entirely change the way this state does business.

The second is the development of a class that none of us are members of. We are readers. There is in this state an enormous number of people who are college degreed, high school degreed, have had some form of education and yet do not read. They do not continue to read books. They don't read for news consumption. Those of us in the news business are very familiar with the fact that almost 60 to 65 per cent of the population today consume their news totally through the electronic media, not using print media at all.

Those are two very startling kinds of populations that are growing in our state. How are we going to cope with people that gain their communication systems and their facts and knowledge in their adulthood through means other than ones that we are using in our education systems, and which we expect them to use as a basis for decision-making in the future? An effort to deal with that is not occurring in this state; it's not occurring in the United States. We are a very special class because we are readers. Most people are not in that class any longer.

William Broyles, Jr.: I sympathize with what you say; you know, I edit a magazine myself. But I suspect, as a sort of au contrairian to this, that a lot of those who are getting their news from television would not in previous generations have been reading or getting any news at all.

Marshall Terry: I'm Marshall Terry; I teach at SMU. This is about education, in a larger sense. One of the panelists used the term "local vision." I think local vision is a great danger for us. Grim as it seems to me, economics is the only real projection for the future, unless it is true that something of the spirit can animate a people. We've heard here today that we Texans are tired of the old mythology, the old frontier icons. They really don't represent us. They embarrass us, and they don't animate us. But it's difficult to build and recognize a new, sustaining belief, if that's what a myth really is. You don't do it by getting up an ad campaign.

There are more than two roads now that are diverging in the woods of our world. Whatever roads Texas takes, they must lead to the larger world. That will be the true transition. Then matters of the spirit, of humility, empathy, understanding, hope for others as well as for ourselves, a sense of shared humanity must be part of that linking of Texas to the world. One of the truly important things that happened in Texas this year was that Rose Mary Catacolos, a poet in San Antonio, had children in the grade schools there write message poems of sympathy and encouragement to the children of the earthquake in Mexico City. Whatever the economic future, that kind of act and understanding must be a major asset of a new Texas, because it helps us to understand also our new diversity and the reality of our situation.

William Broyles, Jr.: I don't necessarily want to choke off the discussion about education, but I want to switch to sort of an all-skate. If anyone has something to say on any of the topics that have or haven't been raised in the course of these discussions, now's the time to speak.

John A. Gronouski: I'm John Gronouski, LBJ School faculty. One of the things that bothers me deeply, not only in Texas but nationally, is that 30 per cent of our kids never get past the seventh, eighth, ninth grade. The dropout problem hasn't been mentioned to my knowledge here, and yet it's a very critical problem over the next quarter-century. As we develop policies nationally that export our manufacturing industry and move into the information age, more and more people are on the junk heap of the job market.

When we talk about unemployment, we're talking about two types. We're talking about the unemployment of people who are competent to take jobs, and we're talking about these other people, thousands and thousands of them, who are on the junk heap of the labor market. They aren't even in the labor market. The pitiful program we have at the federal level we cannot depend on. It is a serious, deeply serious problem that the state must address if we're going to think in terms of economic development in the future.

Ronnie Dugger: Ronnie Dugger, of the *Texas Observer.* A few of us were asked to put ourselves on the spot, so pardon me if, like Marshall, I have written out my thoughts at the lunch hour.

As a Texan I relish the retention of our pride, our history and our specialness as a state and place, and I believe in the work of addressing and trying to reduce social and political problems. The most significant effect of present events, however, is the disappearance of our separateness, the end of our insularity. When our political forebears took Texas away from the Mexicans, there were no telephones or cars. When Lyndon Johnson brought electricity to the Hill Country, there were no televisions or atomic bombs. When we started the *Texas Observer*, there was no integration, there was no civil rights movement, no real environmental movement, no real feminist movement, and certainly no peace movement. Now we are all vulnerable to instant death, delivered through our spreading Texas sky by our fellow human beings in the ocean, and over in the Soviet Union, just as the Soviets are vulnerable to instant death that we might launch from our ocean-ranging submarines or from the silos deep in our own earth.

There is much that is serious, valuable and worthwhile, but there can also be something rather quaint about our meeting here like this, talking about Texas in transition when the overriding question for any of us, Texans or Polynesians, is whether there will be anything to transition to. If we could simply choose what transition to be in, I would choose that while preserving and celebrating and studying our uniqueness and our problems, we stop thinking of ourselves as if our Texas borders in any way protect us from television, refugees, hungry and unemployed Mexican workers, revolutions, tourists—I'm going to use the word—terrorists, domestic monopolies and the international oil cartel, wars in Lebanon or Nicaragua, and missiles in Russia.

Texans, we are Americans. Americans, we are human beings. That is the real transition, and should be. But this is hard, I think, for us to accept and much harder to enjoy, because the essence of our idea of self, of Texas as a culture, is independence. For this key self-idea of ours, the meaning of interdependence is penetration. Or, to be exact, our being penetrated: penetrated by national commerce, penetrated by news we don't want to be, much less read about. Penetrated by foreign people's problems, penetrated by fear of enemy missiles that can penetrate us and explode us.

I would say that the overarching challenge to us in this transition is to try to bring into being among us a new kind of independence. Not the independence of the truculent macho provincial that most of our leading politicians exploit, one way or another, but the independence of the modern realist, an independence that extends to both genders, that is human, and in the whole world, and never nationalistically or nostalgically jingoistic. Among the virtues of the first order in this new kind of independence should be humility. Certainly humility is the virtue most required if we try to foresee, for example, as Mike Gillette and I were saying perhaps I would try to do, the future of Texas politics. Who could foresee in 1977 that the next year Bill Clements would take the state house away from the Democrats, who had owned it since Reconstruction? Who could foresee in 1981 that the next year the state would nevertheless elect to statewide office three Democrats of varying hues of liberalism, and one populist Democrat who's fully worthy of progressive populism's origins out there in the Hill Country about a century ago?

The future shape of Texas politics depends on the world. It depends on what happens to George Bush or Jack Kemp or Bob Dole or Mario Cuomo or Lee "Iacocka" or who else, in the 1988 presidential election, which in turn may well depend on whether the American people awaken or do not awaken to what I take to be the fact that President Reagan is sabotaging this generation's hope for nuclear arms control. Or it may depend on whether the national economy is up or down. Or it may depend, as the 1980 election did, on what some tyrant is doing to kidnapped Americans. Or it may depend on Reagan's war, by then in Nicaragua, and the second major civil convulsion in the last two decades in the United States. It is much less likely to depend on whether we get the Alamo flag back from Mexico than on whether the Sandinista government turns out to be Leninist or not. How could we expect our politics to be separate anymore, when every day of our Texas lives is blown apart by the winds of the world?

But then another of the virtues of the first order in this new kind of Texas consciousness, this Texas-in-the-world consciousness, should be a new kind of calmness. Not the shoot-them-where-they-stand kind of calmness of the Texas Rangers, but a cooling of the legendary Texas temper, a steadiness, an honesty of mind, and the whole, and the true, and the real world. A calmness that rises from fellow feeling as well as strength, as Marshall was saying, from community as well as from individualism.

And there is at least one of the old Texas virtues that still holds its high place in these virtues of the first order, in Texas of the new order, provided it is understood to be a virtue of women as well as of men. And that is courage and the will to act; to see and know the real present, no matter how fast it changes or far it reaches, and go into it fighting.

Martha Cotera: I'm Martha Cotera, publisher of the *Austin Hispanic Directory* and—what else do I do?—consultant to the Benson Latin American Collection here at UT. I wish I had a wonderfully prepared statement like Ronnie. But I do want to say that I totally agree with what he's saying, and that this calmness, as far as I'm concerned, is determined to a great degree by something that I simply do not see in this kind of agenda, which is a facing of the reality of what Texas is: the mainstream of many different cultures, particularly three main cultures, the black, the Hispanic, and the Anglo. And the fact that whatever reality has to be presented in relation to the Hispanic culture, for example, has to come from precious minutes gathered at the floor, and not from the prestige of a podium, to which these gentlemen have been speaking for Texas, and now the newly liberated ladies are a party to, and to which we are still excluded.

But all is well. We're not expecting anybody except Wilhelmina to solve our problems. It's a given that if we have Wilhelmina Delco and Gonzalo Barrientos over there, they have to resolve these problems. No one else seems to have the same responsibilities. Getting Texas to this new realism, that is a real challenge for the future, is the challenge of eradicating this arrogance of power that we see displayed in conferences like this where we are talking about Texas mainstream and it's 99 per cent white and a great percentage male. That is a big number-one challenge, as far as I'm concerned. If we overcame that, a lot of things like sharing educational resources, sharing employment resources and sharing revenues would be resolved.

However, since that is not forthcoming, I guess minorities themselves will have to live up to the challenge of eradicating this high-percentage dropout rate that Gronouski talked about. That is the one thing that's going to affect future revenues, if Texans cannot make it in the work force. We must also work on the equity-sharing business, which is simply sharing taxes and capital with minorities. And I'm not talking about your taxes and your capital; I'm talking about my taxes and my capital.

One of the challenges of Texas is to realize that everybody is taxed, and everybody has to claim that equity. So we are about to claim that equity very fast. I've attended meetings in the Valley where they actually say: "Okay, taxpayers over here, Mexicans over here."

The other equity-sharing process that minorities are claiming—and this is just to advise you ladies and gentlemen out there, not because we expect anybody to come out and give it to us—is a capital sharing. You approach a bank, for example, for a loan. They may have all your money in the world right there, but they're not going to give it to you. This is something again that seems to be our problem and nobody else's, because nobody else is stepping in to solve it. That has a very direct relationship to the development of small businesses, wherein the first line of jobs is created. If minorities don't have access to their own taxes and to their own capital, we have twice as hard a struggle in terms of creating our own economic development. That's a big, big issue.

It is interesting to study the Depression and see who goes down. Unfortunately when they go down they take our capital with them. But those of us that don't have a bunch of capital in there and have it in our own businesses, we can at least survive. I asked this family in Corpus Christi how the Depression impacted them. They said, "Oh, you know,

Mexicans didn't have too much trouble with it, because they didn't keep a lot of the money at the bank and they had their own little businesses and they traded." They traded food for this and the other, so sometimes it works and you can be spared.

Nevertheless, we're getting smarter and we're wanting that equity share. I just want to put you on notice that we're working on that. We're working for our share in tourism bucks also, because that's money. We're not tax exempt from bed-tax money, so now the Hispanic and the black communities are saying, "We have to have that money so we can also promote our market." So we're working on that.

The other challenge that we have to face in Texas is the challenge of race and racism. We are natives here, and we were taken over a hundred and fifty years ago. We're still natives, but when it comes to hiring a Hispanic from Texas or hiring an Anglo from Minneapolis, we're still low person on the totem pole. I'm not saying that we ought to put that kind of prerequisite, "Are you native or are you not?" on the line, but we do have to face a race issue that we're doing ourselves in. More likely than not, the Minneapolis person is going to go right back to Minneapolis, where the Hispanic and black person is right here in the substructural terrain of this great state.

John Odam: I'm John Odam. I would like to pose a concept that has basically four points.

Number one, I use by analogy the movie *Giant,* which I've seen many times. If you haven't seen it lately, I would suggest that you rent the videotape. It's a great social commentary on the state of Texas. You referred to it in the *Texas Monthly* sesquicentennial issue and it's been alluded to here today. The story by Edna Ferber stars Rock Hudson as the cattle baron taken over by the *fifties* J. R., who happened to be Jett Rink. Those two eras have been talked about a lot here, and they are part of the myth. Rock Hudson went into the oil "bidness" that he saw was on the realm. Think about that concept for a second. Paul referred to the seventies being an aberration because of oil prices. We rode a skyrocket here in the state of Texas based upon oil prices that were fixed, predominantly, not by what was happening in the state of Texas, but by what OPEC was doing outside of our control. We were the beneficiaries of it. We all know that. Therefore, Paul, I do think that the seventies were an aberration from the continuum of *Giant,* of the cattle baron and of the Jett Rink era, and oil prices skyrocketing out of sync with the rest of the economy. That is a point to consider.

The third point that we have to consider is that the aberration is unpredictability of oil prices and instability. Susan Longley, who has been monitoring oil prices in the comptroller's office, and I were talking about this problem. It would not surprise anyone if someone were to come in this room and say that OPEC met today in Geneva and dropped the price of oil to eight dollars a barrel. It would not surprise anybody if they came back in and said OPEC decided to jack it up to twenty-five dollars. We in Texas are a part of a larger arena, some of which we don't have any control over. As for the element of instability: it would come as no surprise to anyone if I walked back in this room and said, "I went out and took a break a while ago and I don't know if anyone knows this, but a car bomb just ran into the White House and President Reagan has been killed." It would not come as a surprise to you, because all of us will remember where we were earlier this week when we heard about the bombing of Libya. I happened to be in a meeting with Governor White. I was standing next to the Governor, and someone said, "Did you just hear on the news that the United States is bombing Libya?" My point is simply this: that we live in a condition of instability and unpredictability.

The fourth point is to consider whether or not the state of Texas should continue the momentum and make a sequel. We've had *Rocky I, Rocky II, Rocky III, Rocky IV*; we've had *Rambo I*; we've had *Rambo II.* Maybe we have to make a sequel to *Giant*: *Giant II.* But we live in a world that is unpredictable and unstable. Therefore the question is whether or not we have to pick something—the computer era or whatever it is—that continues this momentum of *Giant* for Texas, or do we have to re-analyze it? Is less better, as Howard Odum suggests? Is the economy in Texas such that we do not necessarily have to make another sequel? It's just a thought that has occurred to me as I have listened to various speakers here. Maybe I'm just totally off in left field, but I'd like anybody else's view on it.

Jan Reid: I'm Jan Reid of *Texas Monthly.* I liked the expression "local vision." I'm also interested in our direction vision. To the extent that we do look afar, we look north, we look west, we look east. But immediately across the river to our south is a shadowy concept that we call Latin America that extends a third of the way around the planet. We know about its savage civil wars, the national economy on the verge of default, and the unemployed millions. But it's also the site of the most inventive literature of our contemporary literatures. Because of our placement, I think in that sense Texas is again a frontier, and I think we need to be looking in that direction far more than our culture has trained us to.

Obviously, it already affects our economy, our agriculture, our education, and to an extent that we may be uncomfortable with, their future is ours.

Richard J. Trabulsi, Jr.: My name is Richard Trabulsi, and I rise to tell you that as of seven-thirty last evening, as I started my journey here, Houston, Texas, still exists. Because it does, we can learn something from it. Houston was referred to earlier as a ghost town. And there are ghosts in Houston; some of them have floated all the way up to the highest levels of Texas heaven and are here on the eighth floor of the LBJ Library today. You just heard from John Odam, Cathy Mincberg, and there are others like them in Houston, Texas.

Houston is suffering its greatest depression since the thirties. It's harder now in Houston than it was then. What we're doing now in Houston and what we will be doing is going to be a lesson for all of Texas. Even those areas of our state that have been prospering are going to enter some difficult times. So I would like to answer some of the specific questions that have been raised here in a very optimistic way, by just pointing out some things that some of my friends are doing.

You can see what Cathy and the school board and school administration in Houston are doing in secondary and primary education. Our magnet program is a model for the entire nation and for other nations as well. Frank Lorenzo, sitting on top of Two Allen Center in downtown Houston, Texas, will direct the nation's largest airline when Texas Air takes over Eastern Air. Frank is like the man of whom Lyndon Johnson is quoted as saying, "He only wanted the land that bordered him." I guess Lorenzo only wants the airlines that he doesn't own. But he's going about it.

The people at Compaq Computer on our Northwest Freeway perhaps are ghosts, but they are creating the fastest-growing industrial enterprise in the United States today by making IBM-compatible desk-top computers.

The people out in our bay area who will be directing the eight billion-dollar space station program are going to add a tremendous amount of technology, education, vibrancy to the entire Texas economy. And they are going to lead us into the new frontiers of space.

My young black friend Milton Carroll, who is thirty-five years old, who worked his way through TSU, has become a millionaire businessman employing Asians and whites and blacks and browns whose only common bond is hard and skilled labor in producing specialty products in his machine shop. He is now chairman of the board of regents of TSU, and he's committed to doing some of the things that we've heard about today, making a special interest university of the first class.

So Houston, Texas, is populated by the right kind of ghosts. I invite all of you who haven't been there to come and see, because Houston, Texas, and I think the state of Texas, will be the most exciting place to be in the new century.

Wilbur J. Cohen: I'm Wilbur Cohen, and I teach at the LBJ School. My life work has been in the field of health, education and welfare, so I'll say a few words about that. But when I was asked to prepare some remarks, I decided that I might give you most by looking in my crystal ball and seeing what Texas would look like twenty-five years from now when we celebrate the 175th anniversary, taking some of the many things that have been talked about here and putting them in the perspective of what Texas will look like as a result of all these forces we've discussed. It's much easier to tell you what Texas will look like twenty-five years from now than to say what it will look like tomorrow.

The first thing which we have tended to overlook is the political revolution that will occur in these twenty-five years. By that time there will have been a woman governor, there will have been a black senator, there will have been a Hispanic senator or congressman, one or more. What we've talked about today in connection with the ethnic problems will have been largely resolved by the minorities having taken political power in the state of Texas and changing the whole relationship with the Anglos and the others in a way that will change the political state of Texas and many of the programs.

The second thing that will happen is we're going to have an income tax and an estate tax and a corporate income tax by twenty-five years from now. Maybe not in the next twenty-four, but probably in the twenty-fifth. And I'm going to comment on it in relation to Representative Delco's point, since one of the three big social issues of the next twenty-five years is the so-called potential conflict between the young and the old. That income tax twenty-five years from now will be earmarked for education for the young and such things as health care for old people. The three big issues will be the conflict between the ethnic groups, the conflict between the rich and the poor, and the conflict between the young and the old. Texas will have to deal with these conflicts in a political sense. They will change a lot of the programs, including taxation and everything else, because we'll have to reconcile them, and I'm very optimistic that we can. One of the ways is to have an income tax that is dedicated, that is earmarked, that everybody shares in. That's one way to deal with it.

Why am I optimistic? We haven't talked about the fact that in twenty-five years when we're celebrating that anniversary, we'll have fusion instead of fission. We'll have other sources of energy. We'll also have desalinization of water at an economic level, and the whole Gulf of Mexico will be available to the state of Texas. So the water problem, in a sense, will be solved. The energy problem will be solved. We're going to have so much more energy and money for education and all these things that we can do, that the pessimism of Reaganomics will be superseded. I should say, first, I don't think Mr. Reagan will be president twenty-five years from now. We will have a per capita income so much greater than we can possibly visualize now that the problem will not be primarily money, it will be the question of priorities that we've talked about, and the allocation of resources in a way that meets the existing social concerns.

Now, I'll say three or four more things. One thing we've overlooked in Texas in connection with both the hospitality and recreation industries is that Texas could be the greatest health industry center in the United States. It could supersede the Mayo and the Ross Loos clinics. Why? Because health expenditures in the next twenty-five years are going to occupy maybe 13 or 14 or even 15 per cent of the gross national product, or the state product. Why? Because every day there are a thousand more people sixty-five and over. Tomorrow morning there are going to be net, one thousand more people sixty-five, the next day one thousand more, the next day one thousand more, the next day one thousand more, the next day one thousand more. And apropos what you said, you're going to have to do something about it.

You're going to have to spend a lot of money. I might say, John Henry Faulk, they're going to be women, too, so you'll have a great time, John Henry.

Life expectancy will be eighty, eighty-five, ninety years; there are going to be more people living to a hundred than ever before. We're going to spend more on health, and we have here in Texas one of the greatest potential industries, and one which Latin Americans use. If you go down to Houston, you'll find more Latin Americans using the hospitals in Houston than you can shake a stick at. We fail to realize that we can expand the health industry better than Massachusetts General in Boston. And that's a very big part of the state income. If we finally get to the time when we change the vote from Tuesday to Saturday or Sunday, so all of these people will vote, that will change the whole internal character of what we do in Texas.

Now, I want to make one final point that's been completely overlooked. I think we've done a good job here talking about Texas obligations and what Texas ought to do, and that's right. But what you've overlooked is that Texas happens to be one of the fifty states of the Union. We haven't yet admitted that today.

William Broyles, Jr.: We call ourselves an affiliate, I think was what Frantz said.

Wilbur J. Cohen: Yes. But the point is, if you study a lot of the state legislation in Texas, it only came about because the federal government forced Texas to do it. Recently we have had a situation where, in the education legislation, the state took initiative, but I could go through the panorama of state legislation that was only enacted because Texas had to take advantage of federal legislation.

If you take my course, you will find out that in 1995 in this country, the federal government is going to start paying a third of the cost of education in the United States, instead of the 6 per cent that it pays today for elementary and secondary, and 20 per cent for higher education. That day must inevitably come, to distribute education among people who are born in other states and come to Texas. It is a problem which Texas can't deal with. It's got to be done through national legislation. When that day comes, there will be an opportunity, built upon whatever experience we have between now and then, for a tremendous expansion in what we've been talking about today, that pulls together the federal government, the state government and the local government in a cooperative relationship. We haven't really talked about that. We've talked about local; we've talked about state. But really the solution to the problem of equity and access is some kind of federal-state-local cooperation that distributes our national resources to the best advantage.

Two other things will happen in 1995 with federal legislation. First, we will subsequently enact something like Mr. Nixon and Mr. Carter wanted that will eliminate poverty in the United States. Nobody seems to be quite surprised about that; I'm amazed. But we will do something that will take all these problems we're talking about, about the poor people, and resolve them in some way through a national program. That's going to change the whole welfare and state programs of the state of Texas in a way that nobody has even contemplated in this meeting.

And the second one will be some kind of national health insurance program that will insure everybody that is not presently insured, so Texas won't have to worry about medical indigency as it did in the last session of the legislature, and so it won't have to put so much of its state resources into health care.

So the point I want to make is that we have to consider when we talk about twenty-five years from now not only what the localities can do, not only what Texas can do, but how Texas as a member of the total Union can have a program for all the people of the United States. There will be a lot of people coming into Texas from other places, and we have to be concerned about their education and their health and their welfare, too.

Rose M. Brewer: I'm Rose Brewer, and I'm a sociologist here at UT. I don't know what I can say after those remarks, because mine are pretty pessimistic. But he's a big optimist.

It is true that Texas is not separate and apart from the rest of the nation, and certainly what happens there will impact on what happens here. But my comment centers on the old growth dynamic versus the new growth dynamic that people have been talking about. Under the old growth dynamic, wealth, income, the whole list of what is available to people was very narrowly distributed. I don't see anything that automatically says that under the new growth dynamic, whether it be centered in oil or in high tech, will mean that this new economic wherewithal will be equally distributed among all people. My charge to the panelists, after listening to them today, is to consider what we can do to assure that the new growth dynamic, whether it be in the form of tourism or whatever, is distributed among all the people of the state. And I really don't think that's an automatic.

Professor Cohen has said that part of the answer is a political one, but we have a problem with political empowerment in the state among minorities. Are we going to guarantee that they have the right to vote? Are we going to guarantee that they have the right to the kinds of representatives that will translate these policy measures into things that will be beneficial to them? These are hard-core questions that we need to spell out and answer in ways that I haven't heard today.

So I don't think fairness and equity are automatically going to come when we say that Texas is going to give up the old myths and embrace new ones around fairness, justice, and those kinds of values. We're very entrenched in an old way of doing things, and it's the charge of those who are in planning, in politics, to think very creatively about how the new growth dynamic is going to filter into the pots, into the households, of all Texans. I don't see that as an automatic.

John Henry Faulk: If I was smart, I would just say amen to Wilbur Cohen and let that be the final word. I'm rejoiced. Now, Ronnie Dugger, all we've got to do is keep her from blowing up between now and twenty-five years from now. It'd be a holiday for all of us.

And I want to thank the gentleman that's announced that Houston's still there.

I thought the best way to have the final word was to introduce you all to several Texans that you haven't heard from yet. They haven't been represented on any of the panels, and their point of view hasn't been represented, because they're folks that I've known ever since I was born. They're poor folks that can't read and write too well. There were an awful lot of them out in South Austin when I was growing up seventy-three years ago. I went up to New York and came back, and there are still an awful lot of them in Texas. For instance, there's my cousin Claude, that just the other day—he can't read and write—announced that he's going to run for the Texas Legislature because he's got hold of some oil land lately, or did make a whole lot of money. And I said, "Cousin Claude, don't you know that illiteracy might be a stumbling block in your political career?" He said, "Johnny, that's the wonderful thing about the Texas Legislature. Ignorance ain't no handicap."

There is old man Walters that I went out to see the other day. He's never been heard from; time's gone past him. I hadn't seen him in forty years, used to play dominoes and checkers with him when I was a little boy. I remember way back there in the old-timey days, right after Pearl Harbor was bombed, the day after Pearl Harbor was bombed. Mr. Roosevelt—and this was how old-timey it was—the President then went before Congress to ask them to declare war. He had just declared war, he'd just gone before a joint House meeting, and they declared war. And I was driving by and I'd heard it on the radio, and I called out to Mr. Walters, "Mr. Walters!" He was sitting there in a wicker chair under a chinaberry tree, taking it easy, which was his wont. And I said, "They've just declared war!" "Sure enough? By God, they've got a nice day fer it!"

I was out there the other day, got out of my car and started to walk up, and Mr. Walters was still sitting in the same old wicker chair, same old droopy overalls on, same old beat-up felt hat, bless his heart. And same chew of tobacco in his jaw, as far as I could tell. And I said, "Mr. Walters. You recognize me?" as I walked up to the gate, because he didn't show the slightest sign. He just looked. And he said, "Sure, I recognize yew, hee hee, John Henry Faulk. Lord have mercy, I'd recognize you anywhar day or night. Son, I'd recognize your ashes in hell."

After that suggestion of where I might spend eternity, I said, "Well, I didn't know, you know, Mr. Walters. By God, I been gone forty years." "Oh, yeah. Ain't missed ye." Well, I got to bragging about all the places I'd been and the people I'd seen and what a high-toned fellow I was, and he said, "You was just who I was ahopin' would come by here one of these times. There's somethin' been frettin' me for the longest, and I hope you can answer it, Johnny. Since President Roosevelt passed away, who's in charge of the De-pression?"

Just this morning I saw Cousin Ed Snodgrass. Cousin Ed Snodgrass is eighty-six years old, and he's been mad for eighty of them. He was six when his momma and daddy told him the South had lost the Civil War. And he was talking about these students that were protesting Ronnie's bombing of Libya, here on the campus. And he'd seen it on TV. He said, "I hope those laws get 'em with billy clubs and take shotguns to 'em; blow 'em into eternity! And run them old perfessers in the schoolhouse with 'em; thow kerosene on it and set fire to the whole bizness!" And I said, "Cousin Ed, now wait a minute. Why would you say something that brutal and terrible?" He said, "Well, somebody's got to put down violence in this country." "Cousin Ed, don't you believe in the right to dissent?" " 'Course I believe in the right to dissent, hit's a sacred American right, and I'll fistfight the man that interferes with my right to dee-sent! What me and Ronald Reagan want to put a stop to is this *criticism.* Criticize, criticize, criticize! Why cain't these old critics leave Ronnie 'lone; let him fight his war in peace?"

And I said, "Well, there's a lot of people scared to death of what's going on." He said, "I know it; that's ignorant. They ain't alooking through the winder of vulnerability that Ronnie is. Ronnie sees what's agoin' on in this here world. He knows them Russians is too tricky to fool with. You old liberals and Democrats are layin' around sayin', 'Oh, we can kill everybody in Russia twenty-five times, and that's a-plenty, and they can't kill us but twelve. So let's lean back, and let's have one of these here arms talks and such as that, and shut down on our a-tomic energy, and all such ugliness as that. Shut down on nuclear wepins.' Johnny, you know what Ronnie understands? He understands that if we have an all-out nuclear hollycaust, and them sneaky Russians has slipped around where they can kill us thirty times, and we're still stuck back there at twenty-five, it'll be too late to run to Ronnie and apologize."

As I say, these are matters that weren't mentioned. These were Texans you didn't hear from. But I do want to congratulate the people who called this conference together. I say this with all sincerity, I have very deep, deep feelings about the open dialogue, rational open dialogue. And today we have heard it in its very best form, and quite appropriately enough, right here where it should be heard: serious, and thoughtful, and penetrating argument carried on. Next year, in September, we will celebrate the bicentennial of our Constitution, when for the first time in the history of all mankind, Meloves, right here on these shores, some men pronounced, "We the people of the United States, in order to form a more perfect Union, establish justice, insure domestic tranquility, provide for the common defense, promote the general welfare, and secure the blessings of liberty to ourselves and our posterity, do ordain and establish this Constitution for the United States of America."

Old Mr. Tom Paine said that every once in a while it's well for us to advert to our first principles. And I thought that it would be proper in the final word to remind you all that what we've done today is to advert to our first principles.

William Broyles, Jr.: Just to bring this to a close, I thought I would just mention something that brings us full circle. We began by commenting and congratulating Larry McMurtry on having won the Pulitzer Prize. I just wanted to remind us of what *Lonesome Dove* is about. It's about two old Texas Rangers on one last cattle drive, and when it is over the Texas they knew is over, and they are over. They didn't know what was going to come next, and Larry McMurtry did not tell us. And it seems to me that we are like those old Texas Rangers, that we are proud of who we are, and not sure of who we will become. We have always been changing, building new worlds on the ruins of old ones. I know we will build a new Texas, more prosperous, more equitable, and more beautiful than ever before. But "it is going to take a heck of a lot of lather to shave that mule." I am glad I came back to help you do it.

held the glamour and romance
trade. For Texas
alike, real
anches, and
repackaged
Red R

EXTENDING THE DIALOGUE. . .

COMMENTARIES

The following section consists of written statements submitted by forum participants after the event. The forum organizers solicited these essays in the belief that some participants would prefer to present their views in writing. There was also a practical consideration: two hours of general discussion is not sufficient time for two hundred people to speak. While the commentaries address topics as diverse as those raised in the dialogue, the emphasis here, as in the forum, is on education and economic development.

GEORGE NORRIS GREEN

Texas is in transition to an unknown future—if there is a future—and I am beginning to doubt that the Texas mystique will survive it. Supposedly in the business and financial world there is a scrambling, go-for-broke quality among Texas entrepreneurs, breaking new fields in business and commerce; they are the modern counterparts of the Texas forefathers who fought Mexicans and Indians, spawned the cattle industry, and discovered oil. The old tools were the horse, the gun, the drilling rig, and of course, courage. The new ones are capital and the guts to use it. But unless people's sense of what is mythic changes, current audacious capitalists simply cannot compare to cattle kings like Charley Goodnight or oil operators like H. L. Hunt. David Nevin in *The Texans* (1967) gave the example of a scrambler who parlayed a shoestring $20,000 of borrowed money into the purchase of 140,000 acres of a ranch eventually enlarged into 220,000 acres. And he noted the careers of the Liedtke brothers, who traded in leases until they founded an oil company that has managed to take over oil companies several times its size.

Goodnight, Hunt, and others were capitalists, too, and the industries cited in these instances are the same as those of yore, but people are seldom captivated by tales of leveraging and creative banking. Even if they were, there is the additional problem of how much longer such entrepreneurship will continue in the old romantic industries. Is there a banker today who would loan a lawyer $20,000 to buy a broken-down ranch? Oil company mergers roll right along, including those perpetrated by Liedtke's Pennzoil, but does anyone regard them as exciting or as adding value to the economy? As the distinctly Texas industries of oil and ranching play out, so do the larger-than-life characters sometimes associated with them. T. R. Fehrenbach observed in *Seven Keys to Texas* (1983) that the land-based Texas economy mostly produces agricultural and mineral products for outside markets. Some forms of wealth are declining, he added, but the Texas faith is that others are still waiting to be found. It's going to be a long wait.

Diversification, especially high tech, is touted by some as the proper course for the Texas economy, but that is the same refrain heard in every state in the union. Jimmy Ling and Bobby Inman have made headlines for high-tech industries, and perhaps they are a bit more colorful than their peers in California and Massachusetts, but are they or their industries the stuff of legends? One can make a better case that high-tech homogenization has befallen the nation and it is permanent. H. Ross Perot resists such typecasting, to be sure, but only because of activities outside the obligations of entrepreneurship. In any event, he is the last of the breed.

Texas's fiction writers are not making the transition,

either. Larry McMurtry has made the most noteworthy effort, insisting that the state's authors concentrate on modern, urban, relevant novels as he has done. Yet his best-known books and his best-received ones are part of the wild west genre. There is still material in western themes, but McMurtry is right in deriding its relevance. Myths do not have to be relevant, but they are stronger when they occur (or reputedly occur) within living memory. How many Texans alive today really had grandfathers who remembered the frontier? Texas's fictional mystique will survive, but in attenuated form.

The Texas mystique is also fading in our schools. "Texas, Our Texas" was probably known to all school children in the thirties, but how many know it today? When Teddy White visited Texas in 1954 he thought that Texas school children were taught about the Battle of the Alamo with far greater intensity than Boston children were taught about Bunker Hill. Perhaps that was true thirty years ago (though I doubt it), but it certainly is not now. The myth holds that history has happened to Texans, both as westerners and southerners, and that they are aware of it, but the average Texas high school graduate does not appear to know a damned thing about the history of his state. Texas's mythic past does not seem to matter anymore.

The political giants of yesteryear were quite as spectacular as the cattle and oil barons. Few states can boast such charismatic founding fathers as Stephen F. Austin and Sam Houston or redoubtable governors like Jim Hogg. Even our flamboyant demagogues—E. J. Davis, Joe Bailey, James Ferguson, W. Lee O'Daniel, Allan Shivers—were matched by only a few southern states. But the governors of the past thirty years have just blended in with run-of-the-mill conservatives elsewhere. Neither Texas nor the U.S. Congress has again experienced anything like the dominance of Lyndon Johnson and Sam Rayburn in the fifties, but that also ended thirty years ago.

It has been argued that the Texas ethos can survive another century as long as the fundamentals of the land do not change, but they are changing. The Texas elan and mystique is being replaced by ordinary efforts to muddle through, and perhaps that is just as well—maybe it will bring us down to earth as we cope with the state's dwindling natural resources and attempt to develop its human resources. Unfortunately, the fact that it took the wholehearted effort of the last of the breed, Ross Perot, to markedly strengthen the state's high school curriculum does not augur well for the chances of the rest of us making a successful transition to the twenty-first century.

LOUIS GRIGAR
I doubt that any of the participants in the recent Sesquicentennial Forum were surprised that most of those who spoke focused on the impact of petroleum on Texas and on the need for educational excellence. The former probably needs little documentation as to the costs and benefits that have accrued to Texans over the decades. Nor can we doubt that our state must seek economic diversification in the future. Unfortunately, time limits and a general agenda limited the discussion of the role of education in our future.

The question of educational excellence and our future as a people is not limited to our state, since a lengthy list of studies and recommendations has come forth recently from national commissions and prominent individuals. All have called on the schools to assume major responsibilities for the future well-being of our citizens. This is not a new or different calling for our educational system. Around the turn of the century, our schools faced the major task of absorbing, educating, and "Americanizing" a vast multitude of immigrants to our shores. Three decades ago, for example, educators were challenged to meet the scientific challenges of Sputnik. During the nearly three decades that I've been associated with public education, our schools have been asked to include a long list of topics in the curriculum, including crime prevention and drug education, metric education, multicultural education, environmental education, and water education. I could extend the list considerably, but I think the ones cited reflect the point that we turn to our schools to address society's problems.

This brings me to the point of suggesting a possible question for a future forum: what is the purpose of our educational system? Lieutenant Governor Hobby, I think, suggested that one major function of our schools is an economic one. Speaking to the State Board of Education at its April meeting, he stated that:

> Our future lies in brainpower. When we demand more of our students and our teachers, it is not so we can brag about Texas's SAT scores. It is because that is the best way our young people can find paying jobs. It is the best way to attract new plants to replace our declining petroleum industry and our faltering farms. It is the *only way* [emphasis mine] we can negotiate the transfer from an economy driven by horsepower to the new economy driven by brainpower.

Such a purpose has a direct relationship to what should be taught, how it should be taught, how future teachers should be prepared, and a host of other educational issues. Others might propose that the training of the intellect is of prime importance and that an economic focus is secondary. Still others may contend that the school's primary function is the transference of the American heritage for good citizenship.

These differing opinions reflect that our education system is a public one, and mirrors the pluralistic nature of that public. It may be timely, given the attention education is receiving, to focus attention on the major purposes of public education and the implications of such proposals. Just what is "excellence?" How is excellence defined and judged? How is excellence achieved? These are questions that could be explored.

I have omitted the question of finance on purpose. Money for education is unquestionably a major consideration, but the funding issue goes to the heart of establishing priorities among a long list of state needs. Perhaps the question of state finance is a topic deserving a forum of its own.

There are a number of individuals who could serve as panelists on a forum on education. Secretary of Education William Bennett, for example, has strongly voiced views on education. Mortimer J. Adler, author of the Paideia Proposal, is another. William T. Coleman, Jr., and Cecily Cannan, co-chairs of the National Science Board Commission, could speak to mathematics, science, and technology education. Another participant could be David P. Gardner, who chaired the National Commission on Excellence in Education. And who could omit the inimitable Ross Perot, whose name is so strongly linked to education reform in Texas?

WILLIAM S. LIVINGSTON

The reason why we must speak today about education is that education is the key to the future of Texas. It is no longer enough to depend upon the traditional economic structures and revenue sources related to agriculture, petroleum, and natural resources. The state must turn its attention to the development of its human resources, and I think we are pretty much agreed on that objective. I question, however, whether we have faced the full implications of that reorientation.

If high tech is to be our future, we must begin now to strengthen education at all levels. Texas ranks forty-fifth out of the fifty states in average SAT scores. In 1976 we were ten points below the national average, and in 1985 that difference had increased to twenty-eight points. The Perot Commission and H.B. 72 were steps in the right direction, but we still have a long way to go.

It is not enough, however, to strengthen primary and secondary schools. What is equally urgent is the need to support higher education. Above all, the state must strengthen its comprehensive, research-oriented institutions, for it is in them that the key to the future resides. I do not depreciate the mission or the importance of the ordinary state university, but the mission of the research-oriented university is different. The future of Texas lies not only in educating its citizens but in developing its research capacity to sustain an economy that will be increasingly technologically sophisticated; that task has to be performed in the research universities.

Basic research is directly related to the prosperity of the state. The vast preponderance of the nation's research is done in the universities, not in corporate or public laboratories. There are numerous programs at the University of Texas alone that promise to change our lifestyle and our economic future—programs related to cancer, computers, and culture; studies on the origins of human writing, how children learn to read, and on and on. In 1984-85 the University received one hundred and four million dollars in external research grants and contracts. There is a multiplier effect related to those research dollars which fed something over three hundred million dollars into the Texas economy. Moreover, the one hundred and four million dollars in external support was generated by an initial infusion of state funds on the order of twenty million dollars. That means there was approximately a five-to-one return on our investment. Research in the research-oriented universities helps Texas firms become more competitive in the market and helps attract new business to the state. There is a direct link between research, economic development, and the prosperity of our citizens.

If the state's research universities are to help develop a technologically sophisticated economy, several things have to happen. They must be managed through funding formulas that differentiate them from other institutions of higher education. The state must find different ways of funding organized research. The state must commit itself to an expanded program of support for graduate students. The state must find new ways of handling indirect costs and purchasing procedures. The state must encourage, not restrain, its comprehensive, research-oriented universities, which are too often over-regulated and under-supported. Only thus can the future be assured.

The task of reorienting the economy and the revenue structure is one that must command the concern of all our leaders. It is not my responsibility to suggest particular ways and means. I can properly say, however, that finger-pointing won't do it. An attack on "local funds" won't do it. Dismantling the PUF won't do it. A penny on the sales tax won't do it. Indeed, an exclusive concentration on "high tech" won't do it. What's needed is not merely computer science and microelectronics but a new emphasis on a broad range of specialties in science and engineering and a renewed emphasis on the humanities and the liberal arts.

What is needed is an educated citizenry, not merely a trained citizenry—if for no other reason than that the technology itself will keep changing. People will be changing jobs and changing specialties. They must not only be trainable but re-trainable; educated, not merely well drilled. As Ross Perot has said, "We can't afford to produce a population of technological robots."

Massachusetts and California faced this same sort of problem some twenty years ago and addressed it with large infusions of resources into higher education. The result was Silicon Valley and Highway 128. Massachusetts is a state with few natural resources except an educated citizenry, but it has an unemployment rate of 4.4 per cent as compared with Texas's 8.4 per cent. Texas is twenty years behind those states in its investment in research and graduate education, and Texas now urgently needs a similar long-term investment in its human resources and in its future. In 1985-86, higher education in Texas received virtually a zero increase in appropriated funds, which made it dead last among the fifty states. At the same time six states (including California and Massachusetts!) increased their support for higher education by more than 30 per cent. Moreover, twelve states increased such support by more than 20 per cent. Texas cannot afford to postpone its own commitment. The universities of the state cannot produce a citizenry that is educated and technologically sophisticated without a significant infusion of financial support.

The people of Texas recognize the urgent need for improvements in education, both public and private, both secondary and post-secondary, both graduate and undergraduate. The Select Committee on Higher Education may very well take steps comparable to those of the Perot Commission and H.B. 72. The difficulty is that while we are all in favor of education and united in proclaiming that it is the key to the future, we do not say the same thing when we are talking about taxes, revenues, and appropriations. Too many people in public life pay lip service to higher education, but when they turn to revenues and appropriations, they talk about retrenchments, constraints, and the political virtue of no new taxes—frequently adding that education must share its part of the burden. I put it to you that we cannot have it both ways. We need statesmanlike responses and the courage to face the future. History and posterity will judge us for the decisions we make about these hard but critical priorities.

ROLAND BOYD

In William Broyles's portion of the forum, Felicia Jeter said, "I want responses from this group. How can we get economic development started? I want specifics." I responded by saying we should develop our water resources. I did not feel that I should give the specifics then. I give them now. We on the East Fork of the Trinity River watershed in 1950 prevailed on the Texas Legislature to create the North Texas Municipal Water District out of ten small suburban cities to the north and east of Dallas. At that time those cities had a combined total population of 33,000. Now they have a combined total population of 504,000. I attach a schedule of growth for each of those cities (attachment 1). Collin County, where Lavon Lake is located, at that time had a total assessed property valuation of twenty-five million dollars. Now Collin County has a total assessed valuation of between thirteen and fifteen billion dollars. We have built new hospitals, new churches, new homes, new courthouses, new city halls, new museums, new golf courses and community centers. Now our young people do not leave home after college, as they did previously.

Of the 954 rural water supply corporations in the state of Texas, 84 per cent do not have an adequate supply for the year 2010. Major surface lakes are the solution to this problem. Nature provided very few natural sites for major surface lakes, and these are being destroyed by development at an alarming rate. We must acquire all remaining natural sites now. They can be kept as parks or wildlife areas until they are needed for drinking water. Our economic development has been stifled by misguided, no-growth environmentalists. The Texas Committee on Natural Resources stopped the construction of Cooper Reservoir, our next source of water, in May 1971. It took twelve years to remove that injunction. This twelve-year delay added over one hundred million dollars to the direct cost of Cooper Reservoir. These people have given the snail darter, the nutmeg hickory tree, the grizzly bear, the coyote and the Concho River snake dominion over man. We must reverse this waste. To do this, we have organized in the District of Columbia a National Association of Drinking Water for Human Beings, Inc., a nonprofit, nonpolitical, nonpartisan, educational institution. We intend to organize from the bottom up, starting with the local chambers of commerce (there are 530), the mayors and city councils (there are 1,100), the local school boards (there are 1,083), the county courthouses (there are 254), and the local soil and water conservation boards (there are 198). In 1977, the three pro-water organizations had a total combined annual budget of five hundred and fifty thousand dollars. Eleven of the environmental groups had a combined annual budget of forty-one million dollars (attachment 2). The Wildlife Federation had an annual potential of seventeen million dollars. We do not need this kind of money. Since we are a 90 per cent-plus majority, we can take two million dollars annually and buy the sites and get the water resources of our state developed. I attach a list of the different sources that should provide the money.

1. Water lawyers;
2. Municipal bond lawyers;
3. Investment bankers;

4. Civil engineers engaged in designing water projects and facilities;
5. Contractors who build water facilities;
6. Pipe manufacturers;
7. Meter manufacturers;
8. Pump manufacturers;
9. Chemical manufacturers and suppliers;
10. Water districts and people who receive their livelihood from the districts;
11. 1100 cities—254 counties;
12. Paid managers of water supply corporations;
13. A few pennies' tax on customers put on monthly bills;
14. Foundations.

Attachment 1

Population of the Eleven Member Cities,
North Texas Municipal Water District

CITY	1950	1960	1970	1980	1985*	1950–1985 % INCREASE
Farmersville	1,949	2,021	2,236	2,360	2,650	35.97
Forney	1,418	1,544	1,725	2,483	3,300	132.72
Garland	10,291	38,501	80,659	138,857	171,500	1,566.50
McKinney	10,525	13,763	14,773	16,256	19,300	83.37
Mesquite	1,684	27,526	55,134	67,053	89,500	5,214.73
Plano	2,126	3,695	17,600	72,331	110,450	5,095.20
Princeton	531	594	1,064	3,408	2,700	408.47
Richardson	1,289	16,810	48,582	72,496	89,500	6,843.37
Rockwall	1,499	2,166	2,905	5,939	9,050	503.73
Royse City	1,243	1,274	1,496	1,566	1,850	48.83
Wylie	1,292	1,804	2,553	3,152	4,800	271.52
TOTAL	33,847	109,698	228,727	385,901	504,600	1,390.83

*NTCOG estimates
Source: Official Census Records

Attachment 2

Environmental Movement Financing, 1977

Organization	Membership	Annual Budget
Pro Water:		
Texas Water Conservation Association		$150,000.00
Water Resources Congress		180,000.00
Ntl. Water Resources Association		220,000.00
		550,000.00
Opposition:		
Environmental Defense Fund	44,000	1.6 million
Friends of the Earth	22,000	670,000.00
National Audubon Society	350,000	8 million
National Parks & Conservation Assoc.	45,000	950,000.00
National Wildlife Federation	3.5 million	17 million
Natural Resources Defense Council	35,000	1.9 million
Nature Conservancy	28,000	3.5 million
Massachusetts Audubon Society	25,000	2.4 million
Sierra Club	163,000	3 million
Izaak Walton League	53,000	400,000.00
Wilderness Society	75,000	1.7 million
	4,340,000	$41,120,000.00
Opposition Foundations (do not solicit members):		
Conservation Foundation		$1.5 million
Environmental Policy Center		250,000.00
Scientists Institute for Public Information		400,000.00
Worldwatch Institute		500,000.00
		$2,650,000.00

Source: Records filed in compliance with federal election law

JOHN EDWARD WEEMS

With weather such an important factor in Texas, I am rather surprised that the subject did not receive more prominent discussion in the forum. Although a climatologist or a meteorologist could discuss the topic more specifically, my research on weather, which began in 1956, has convinced me that weather has influenced Texas development vitally and will continue to do so, possibly beyond the imaginations of otherwise astute observers.

Weather is indeed the word to use, of course, and not climate. Texas is so extensive it has no single climate, and the weather certainly can differ from place to place. Parts of Texas can wither in extended droughts while at the same time others suffer catastrophic floods.

Weather can help explain much Texas history. Probably a major reason that many parts of East Texas seem, even today, to have been lifted from the Deep South is that southerners immigrating into Texas long ago found *that* particular climate and countryside to their liking, since it seemed like home, and they stayed even when other land opened westward. In East Texas they found usually abundant rainfall and trees and rivers.

Weather extremes peculiar to Texas probably have contributed to the Texas propensity for exaggeration. Bizarre weather stories have become cliches, but Texas indeed offers bizarre weather even without the exaggeration. The violence of their weather possibly has rubbed off on numbers of Texans—or at least some outsiders of sophistication might think so from reading newspaper accounts of Saturday night violence.

More mention of weather could have gone into the discussion of how Texas has become what it is today, and certainly weather could have figured in the speculations about tomorrow's Texas. So much material for discussion is available, in fact, that the matter could be a single topic for another forum. Topics for such a discussion might be the development of plants that could better survive drought, the enactment of building codes along the Gulf Coast that would enhance chances of construction there withstanding the pounding of hurricanes, and methods of building residences and other structures with sufficient strength to greatly lessen the damage from tornadoes—methods available at this very moment.

Admittedly, some of these subjects would not have belonged in the "Texas in Transition" discussion, but more emphasis on water certainly would have fit. Texas *does* have a current water plan, of course, and it was mentioned, if only briefly, along with a few other problems stemming from the aridity of much of the state. In the future, however, much more public attention will be focused on water, especially if the population expands to the degree that many predict. Unless some continuing problems are solved soon, water will limit the state's growth potential.

To discuss just one example: San Angelo, a city with eighty thousand or so residents, is experiencing water-shortage troubles as this is being written (although by the time this is read, floods might have changed the situation, at least temporarily). The levels of Lake Nasworthy and other reservoirs there are so low that water has had to be piped in—all of which has resulted in drinking water that some citizens say tastes as if it had been filtered through cow chips. Nevertheless, the people there at least have water, though I have heard one observer remark that the city might as well forget about vast growth; it cannot even take care of today's population, and could not even if every drop of rain were saved.

I suspect that this is an exaggeration. If crowded Southern California can get water, Texas should be able to have water by exerting enough effort. However, San Angelo *is* the same city where firemen once fought a blaze on a lake, when vegetation left poking out of a dry bed caught fire. A nationally popular piece of music, "Fire on the Lake," reputedly evolved from that incident. Fortunately, the firemen had enough water (or chemicals) to do their job, but what of the future—there and elsewhere in Texas.

DORMAN WINFREY

An area of change in Texas has been the movement of a great many persons from large cities to small towns. After these persons left the small towns to go to the city during the Second World War, they have in many instances "done well" and are now returning to their earlier homes.

These persons are making their mark on the towns and communities of their origin. Many run for public office, hold positions of importance, and make contributions of significance to the localities to which they have returned. They bring with them a great deal of talent gained from their former employment in the city.

The changes in small Texas communities were very noticeable in the 1980 Census. In a Texas A&M Department of Rural Sociology technical report the authors state:

> Even more startling is the level of change in the smallest communities in Texas. The population in places of less than one thousand grew by 46 per cent, and the mean percentage change (average percentage change) for such places was 58 per cent. These rates are nearly twice those for any other category. In addition, when growth in places within this [less-than-one thousand] population category is analyzed further, it is evident that the smallest places grew the fastest.

In modern times the small town continues to provide a large share of successful Texans: Governor Mark White (Henderson), Van Cliburn (Kilgore), Larry McMurtry (Archer City), Tom Bradley (Calvert). Rural America has historically contributed significantly to the leadership pool, but the rural source from which came men and women with this unique background had been in decline. In Texas State Data Center Report Number 2, Series 1985, *The Population of Texas: An Overview of Texas Population Change 1970-1980*, the authors observe that:

> The Texas rural population grew steadily during the late 1800s and the early 1900s before peaking in 1940 at

> 3.5 million. The number of rural residents then declined until 1970, before increasing to 2,896,174 persons in 1980. The 1980 figure was 17 per cent lower than the number of rural inhabitants prior to World War II but 28 per cent more than in 1970.

"Texas Tomorrow" may have a brighter future if the small town continues to grow and prosper, a trend that seems likely for East Texas and communities near metropolitan areas, at least. Such growth would be the preference of nearly half of Americans, according to a recent Gallup poll. If this trend continues, rural Texas is likely to benefit from the optimism inherent in growth and renewal, as opposed to the debilitating impact population loss can have on a community's spirit.

HOWARD FALKENBERG

Texas is more than a state; it is a state of mind. One factor in this is that our values are different, perhaps because we remain closer to our agrarian roots. As a communicator and economic developer, I believe it is our values, nurtured by our special history and our sense of destiny, that will permit us to meet the challenges of the transition and well beyond into our future.

While I have confidence and an optimistic spirit about our ability to respond to challenge, I would suggest that there is an issue in our future that was little addressed at the forum. That issue is the readjustment in attitude and structure that will follow the full implementation of Gramm-Rudman. I think this single measure will force as wrenching a shift as anything else suggested.

The fact is that Texas will be in a better position than most because we understand the concept of balanced budget better in practical application, and because our value system will permit us to make the effort to adapt, perhaps more easily than others will be able to do.

In fact, by reason of our "state of mind" attributes of hard work, courage, initiative and spirit, combined with an improving base of education, we can thrive. The initial readjustment will be incredibly difficult, however. It will drive people out of business, add to the agonies of many of our citizens, reduce public services and constrain our life-style—to mention just a few implications of Gramm-Rudman. The long-term benefits may outweigh the temporary dislocations, but I think the issue is certainly serious and worthy of discussion and planning as we look ahead to the future of Texas.

FREDERICK WILLIAMS

Although "reindustrialization," "diversification," "technology," and "computers" received their share of mention in the many excellent contributions about the future of our state, there was no mention of "information society," a current concept that could illuminate a few of our options for seeing our state through the current transition.

Much of the best thinking about the concept of an information society dates from the late sixties in the writings of Harvard sociologist Daniel Bell. (His most comprehensive statement was published in 1976 in *The Coming of Post-Industrial Society*.) Essentially Bell theorized that economies mature through phases where a dependence upon the land as a source of wealth ("preindustrial") is succeeded by the ability to create wealth from machines ("industrial"), which in turn may evolve into what Bell calls a "post-industrial" phase. In this phase, of particular relevance to Texas, the main source of wealth goes beyond the land and manufacturing to capitalize upon the generation and use of *information*.

A primary form of an information industry is one specializing in research and development, a major example of which would be the Microelectronics and Computer Technology Corporation. Also included among primary information businesses are those specializing in the production of goods or services related to information processing (e.g., IBM, Texas Instruments, EDS, and in some major respects, Southwestern Bell). These are the most visible growth industries of an information society, and except for the recent slump in microelectronics, experience is bearing this out. And, of course, the foregoing are the types of industries targeted for the reindustrialization of Texas.

But there is more to this theory than just the growth of "primary" information industries. There is also the secondary sector of the information economy where traditional businesses are made more productive by investments in information technologies. The acquisition of Electronic Data Services by General Motors is a key example. Moreover, if you examine most contemporary businesses, even down to the smallest, there have been recent investments in information technologies. Although nobody knows the exact figures, there is considerable reason to believe that investments in this secondary sector and the impact of those investments may far outdistance the more visible and dramatic Silicon Valley-type companies. In the Texas perspective, therefore, we should pay as much heed to revitalizing existing industries as to attracting new ones.

Urban examples of technology investment are relatively well known: computer-aided design and manufacturing, management information systems, office automation, "smart" buildings and the like. Although these are important to a Texas in transition, there are also less well known examples of revitalization of rural businesses by information technology investments. Some examples from our research files include:

Iowa Beef processors significantly increased their profitability by installing mobile radio and satellite terminals to allow direct communication between buyers on the road and their headquarters.

In several projects, satellite distribution of commodity news allows farmers to make better and faster decisions about when and where to sell their produce.

There are studies of how new computer and telecommunication networks linking soil moisture sensors to irrigation systems can offer dramatic advances in water conservation.

After installation of a satellite earth station, a fish packing plant in Atka, Alaska, improved its profitability. The manager was able to communicate directly with headquarters in Seattle to determine which types of seafood were in greatest demand or bringing the highest price.

Using telecommunications networks, credit card statements and telephone catalog orders can now be processed much more rapidly in direct data form in small towns far from major commercial centers.

Electronic funds transfer systems cut the costs of money-handling, giving the rural bank many of the advantages of the urban institution.

Hewlitt-Packard has improved its managerial effectiveness and cut travel costs through use of an in-house satellite teleconferencing network for meetings of technical staff from widely separated plants in California, Idaho and Colorado.

In Alaska, Appalachia, and the Southwestern U.S., paramedical health workers have been able to contact physicians to assist in diagnosis and treatment of rural patients. Data including chest sounds, EKGs and medical records can be transmitted over telephone lines.

A current New Zealand project indicates that the major lamb business in that country could probably double its profitability through use of computers to "track" inventory and an information network to link sales efforts with major world markets.

The impact of information technologies extends to public services as well as to business, two main examples of which are the operation of government and the delivery of education. As in the operation of business, we should expect our public agencies and departments to increase their productivity through implementation of technologies. We should ask whether the major agencies of our state government are giving this prospect the attention it deserves. (Not once in the current flurry of reaction to Governor White's required budget cuts have I read of any agency head who plans to make those cuts through the use of technologies for increasing productivity. Yes, computers can be notorious money-wasters, but that is a management problem, not a technological one.)

Information technologies can also assist us in the revitalization of public education in Texas. Unfortunately, here, as well as in most parts of the country, educators have an especially poor record for technology implementation. Classes are taught much the way they have been for the last half-century, a situation that sooner or later will have to change as the constantly rising cost of traditional forms of instruction exceeds the ability of property taxes to pay the bill. Despite the attention given small computers in the classroom, very little has been done to use them to improve the teaching of basic subjects.

The growing experience with new telecommunications technologies is also extending to health care delivery, emergency warning systems, and public information networks, all as accessible to the rural citizen as the urban one.

The public dimension of the information society also extends to the various "information utilities," especially the public telephone network. Granted that antitrust actions and the divestiture of the Bell Telephone system have made it difficult for telephone companies to plot their future, our own Southwestern Bell, according to the *Wall Street Journal*, has made the least successful transition. We should have high expectations from the company that owns the major telecommunications networks of our state. By the same token, our Public Utilities Commission fails to encourage an atmosphere for investment with its one-dimensional concentration on rate restriction. If Texas is to be attractive to information industries, it will have to make—or encourage to be made—major investments in the telecommunications infrastructure. This is not likely to happen until Southwestern Bell and the PUC join the information age.

In all, the potential of Texas as an information society is considerable. We have had the benefits of information technology industries (Tracor, Texas Instruments, Tandy) well before these types of businesses became popular. We have considerable telecommunications expertise in this state (some of the best telecommunications engineers come from the oil business.) And we have the rapidly growing information technology talents being assembled by MCC and the University of Texas at Austin.

But perhaps best of all, we may have the edge in this country on where we wish to go. California has often been mentioned by other contributors as an example of success with new industries. Yet I would like to say, as a resident of California for the last decade as well as a researcher into information age concepts, that Silicon Valley is not a statewide phenomena. It is local and despite its spectacular growth, the impact on the state has been modest. In Texas we can encourage the growth of an information economy that benefits more than a group of entrepreneurs; in particular we can further encourage the aforementioned secondary sector. There is no other state in the Union that has the team effort that we have now in Texas between government and business. Added to our information technology resources, this may just give us that needed competitive edge.

RICHARD K. CHEN

The 150th birthday of Texas becomes more colorful as more minority groups take part in celebrations everywhere in Texas.

The Oriental population is growing in Texas. More and more job opportunities have been created by these people, who put their lifetime investment here in the Lone Star State. As the economy falters, all are in the same boat. We, like other Texans, like to share our experiences and feelings with everybody. But communication between local Oriental communities and state government is not yet open. We would like to see more exchange of opinions in the future, not only on politics, but also on education, economics, et cetera. The existence of the Oriental community and culture cannot be ignored. Hopefully, through more communication and exchange, we can work together for a better future.

MICHAEL S. HVEZDOS

Mayor Henry Cisneros of San Antonio remarked on the need to change our mind-set from the cowboy and oil culture of Texas—the rugged frontier self-reliant image portrayed to the world. Instead, he said, we need to look at improving the service industry in Texas.

Many businesses may require such an attitude adjustment, but we should not discourage the Texas entrepreneurial spirit. If tourism is Texas's third largest industry, that is largely because of the Texas image. That's what tourists expect and want to see. Towns, cities and individual entrepreneurs can use this perceived identity to generate further tourism while raking in the profits. What they do need is some good marketing advice.

Lest we forget, environmental protection is closely tied to tourism and Texas does not have a good record in the area. It needs much more attention.

Development of water resources is closely allied with tourism and environmental protection. Lake O' the Pines, in East Texas, had four and a half million visitors in 1985, according to Corps of Engineers estimates. The tourist/recreational industry can flourish through development of additional reservoirs which also serve as adequate water supplies for agriculture, cities and industries. A major industrial attractor, water can be the oil of the future for Texas.

California was repeatedly cited during the forum as a model for a state education system. Florida may be worthy of study to learn from their marketing techniques in attracting industry and from their strong environmental protection skills. Tampa, in particular, has been successful in attracting corporate headquarters and electronic industries—both providing nonpolluting state economic growth. Texas offers all the same advantages of Florida except strong environmental protection laws and enforcement.

While, as Mayor Cisneros pointed out, towns and cities need to concentrate on establishing a business climate conducive to attracting small businesses and industries, we should not ignore the Saturn and Toyota plant opportunities which come our way, as was implied. With stronger state support, we could be successful in attracting those major industries, too.

Agriculture Commissioner Jim Hightower's comments on self-marketing and local packaging of agricultural products also apply to other Texas products. Instead of shipping Texas-produced chemicals to another state for packaging, let's package them in Texas and employ Texans while keeping the profits in the state. Let's employ Texas transportation to ship them where needed. It doesn't make sense for our Gulf Coast shrimpers to sell their catch to a company in Louisiana to be packaged and then brought back into Texas in Louisiana trucks to be sold to Texas grocers and restaurants. Let's do it all in Texas, keep the money at home and improve our business/industry development and our job market in the process.

Another business and economic weakness is the failure of the state to establish trade offices in foreign countries to help market Texas products, including agricultural products. Other states are doing this quite successfully; we lag far behind. It requires an investment that would be worthwhile in the long run.

Growing minority populations present challenges and opportunities on educational, cultural, economic, social and political fronts. Major problems loom in social services, health care, law enforcement and allied areas. Illegal immigration problems, adequate prisons, indigent care, mental health care, drug trafficking, care for the elderly and other quality-of-life issues must be addressed now.

The forum's focus on education highlighted one key point: *Texas must produce a literate workforce.*

In higher education, there are few opportunities for graduate degree work in East and Northeast Texas. People travel from Longview to Shreveport, Louisiana, or to Nacogdoches, Tyler, Commerce and Dallas to work on master's and doctoral programs, but the available degree fields are extremely limited. As in El Paso, Longview and East Texas need the state education system's graduate programs to support our economic, social and cultural progress. Not everyone can move to Austin or College Station to acquire this education. Nor can they afford enrollment in a private university. The lack of local higher education opportunities greatly affects the ability of a town or city to attract corporate headquarters and white-collar industry. Expansion of these educational opportunities must be a major priority throughout the state.

We are making some inroads into improving public schools and the quality of teachers. While not perfect, H.B. 72 has provided progress in this area. More is needed. Tougher requirements for attaining teaching credentials and even higher teacher salaries are needed to attract the brightest and the best. Also, more must be done to decentralize mandatory or state-directed instruction to allow teachers more flexibility in planning for the needs of their students at the local level. Let's keep the momentum going in this area.

Blue-collar education is also important. Texas State Technical Institute continues to expand into areas where vocational skills are needed, providing instruction for skills in which there are local employment shortages. They also assess future employment needs, provide retraining programs and help secure a base of workers in the local communities. We need more of this type of thinking.

Texas is in transition, but the self-pride, entrepreneurial spirit and forward thinking of Texans—as evidenced by participants in the Sesquicentennial Forum—will overcome the adversities and problems facing our state. I was greatly encouraged to learn from the forum panelists and participants that determined men and women of Texas are identifying these problems and working toward solutions by which we all shall benefit.

IMAGES OF TEXAS IN TRANSITION

Photographs document change in ways that words cannot. The following photographs depict some of the transformations Texas and Texans have undergone during this century, as well as some of the events that brought about these changes: the Great Depression, the rise of the oil industry, World War II, the civil rights and women's movements, and the advent of the electronic age. We see, too, the emergence of cities, the evolution of modern political campaigning, and shifts in economic and social concerns.

Yet these photographs also reveal something else about Texas. While some features of the state's heritage have disappeared, others remain embedded in the Texas culture and identity. Thus Texans retain their cowboy mystique through country-western music and their historic propensity for glory and combat through football. The images of an earlier Texas lead one to speculate on those of our present era. How dated will these scenes of the Texas Senate, the detention of illegal aliens, and a student at a computer keyboard seem in the year 2000?

Galveston's Crystal Palace and Murdoch's Bath House in the late 1910s. (Rosenberg Library, Galveston.)

A run on San Antonio's City Central Bank during the Depression. (The *Light* Collection, Institute of Texan Cultures.)

Celebrating V-J Day in Dallas. (The Hayes for the *Dallas Times Herald*, Texas/Dallas History and Archives Division, Dallas Public Library.)

Picketing Dallas's segregated Melba Theater in 1954. (R.C. Hickman Collection, Eugene C. Barker Texas History Center.)

Oil as a way of life in Kilgore in the late 1930s. (Wendell McRae, Eugene C. Barker Texas History Center.)

Houston's Main Street in the 1940s. (Eugene C. Barker Texas History Center.)

A scene from the Kokernot Ranch in 1939. (Eugene C. Barker Texas History Center.)

Bob Wills, the "King of Western Swing," and the Texas Playboys in 1941. (Bob Wills Museum, Fort Worth, Texas.)

Maury Maverick addresses a San Antonio crowd circa 1938. (Eugene C. Barker Texas History Center.)

Allan Shivers speaks to a Fourth of July courthouse crowd in Belton. (Russell Lee Collection, Eugene C. Barker Texas History Center.)

Television enters Texas politics in a Ralph Yarborough campaign. (Russell Lee Collection, Eugene C. Barker Texas History Center.)

Vice President Lyndon Johnson and Governor John Connally attend a benefit for Houston's Alley Theatre, August 12, 1963. (Jim Cox Collection, LBJ Library.)

Earl Campbell, the Tyler Rose, in high gear for UT Austin against SMU, 1977. (Tom Lankes, *Austin American-Statesman*.)

Texas women play leading roles at the National Women's Conference in Houston, November 1977. (Ave Bonar.)

A Texas Farmworkers Union march from Muleshoe to Austin in 1979. (Alan Pogue.)

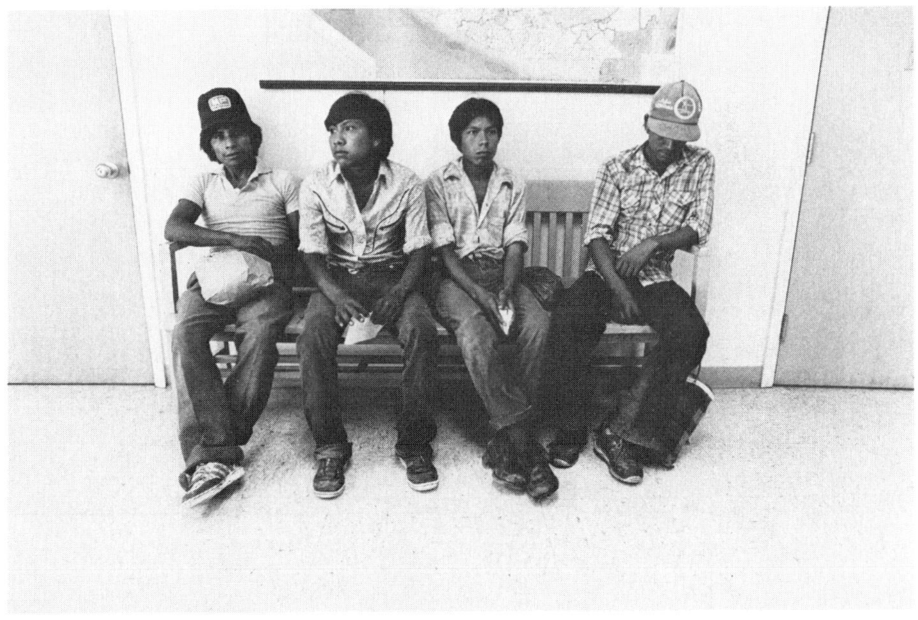

Illegal aliens are detained in Brownsville in 1986. (Ave Bonar.)

Members of the Texas Senate confer with presiding officer Lieutenant Governor Bill Hobby. (Alan Pogue, 1985.)

Jones Rig No. 51, near Albany, Texas. (Rick Williams.)

Texas education in the 1980s. (Texas Education Agency.)

Texas Centennial Exposition in Dallas, 1936. (Texas/Dallas History and Archives Division, Dallas Public Library.)

New Year's Eve Sesquicentennial Celebration in Dallas, 1985. (Bill Canada.)

THE JOURNALISTS' VIEWS

This section presents a selection of newspaper and magazine articles generated by the Texas in Transition forum. They are included in this volume not only to bring together news coverage of the event for the purpose of documentation, but also to add another dimension to the forum's discourse. Many of the state's leading journalists and communicators were invited as forum participants in the hope that they would extend the dialogue to a wider audience through their own writings, speeches, and conversations. As the following selections demonstrate, a number of them have done so.

GREGORY CURTIS, *Texas Monthly*, "Behind the Lines" (June, 1986)
Let's suppose that you, like the majority of Texans, are for no pass, no play. Let's suppose that you, like the majority of Texans, are for competency testing of both teachers and students, smaller classes, and paying teachers more money. Let's say that not only do you support those new laws but, unlike the majority of Texans, you also want to work to make sure those reforms remain in force or perhaps are even expanded. Whom would you call? Where would you go?

I asked these questions of Cathy Mincberg, a member of the board of the Houston Independent School District. She thought for a moment, and then thought for a moment longer. "I guess there's no one," she said. "I can't think of any group that is organized to show support for the educational reforms. And we are in danger of losing them."

I had sought her out after hearing her ask a few incisive questions at the end of a seminar called "Texas in Transition" at the University of Texas. (It was sponsored by the University, the Lyndon Baines Johnson School of Public Affairs, the LBJ Library, and *Texas Monthly*.) Although they were from various backgrounds, the speakers all made similar comments about the importance of education to the future of Texas, and some of their remarks are worth repeating.

Larry McMurtry, novelist and this year's winner of the Pulitzer Prize: "What distinguishes Texas is its *human* energies that have changed the state from rural to urban. But energy alone won't produce a culture. We are an optimistic state in an optimistic nation, and with good reason. But society, in fact, isn't naturally progressive. We may have reached a point where we have to plumb our psyches in order to progress."

Henry Cisneros, mayor of San Antonio and president of the National League of Cities: "Texas has relied on nature. Meanwhile, California has relied on its people and built a great university."

Joe B. Frantz, recently retired after forty years on the history faculty of the University of Texas and the former head of the Texas State Historical Association: "Texas is like an attractive, troublesome, and immature person who gets an inheritance—ranching—and then gets a second one—oil—and now has to grow up and get to work."

Scott Bennett, management consultant and columnist for the *Dallas Morning News*, began with a defense of Allan Shivers, Lyndon Johnson, and the past leadership of Texas, and said that on the whole, they had been good for business and that was good for Texas. But Bennett saw certain failures in the Texas business mentality: "Sometimes it's too practical for its own good. It won't insist upon schools' teaching the intellectual dimension of life. If the East has dominated policy in the country, it's because it has had no competition. We did not enter the fray. We did not invest enough in schools to develop ideas. As for the future, I'm worried about the entry of people on the fringe into the two-party system, people with narrow agendas who force out the mainstream. With the Reagan revolution, we have had a return to states' responsibilities, and the state may not be able to meet those responsibilities with less government. Too much government at the federal level is not always too much at the local level."

David Prindle, associate professor of political science at the University of Texas, winner of the Allan Shivers Teaching Award, and author of a history of the Texas Railroad Commission, explained that Texas had managed the oil industry to maximize prosperity by keeping the price high, keeping the money in Texas, and spreading the money around the state: "Thus, it was not oil itself but intelligent public policy that produced prosperity in Texas. Today we don't have an oil price crisis so much as a public policy crisis. New England has no natural resources, yet it now has the lowest unemployment rate in the country. Why? Because it emphasized education and used a state income tax to pay for public needs."

Bernard L. Weinstein, director of the Center for Enterprising at Southern Methodist University and chairman of the Texas Economic Policy Advisory Council: "The oil card has been played. For the future, we should redo the tax system and concentrate on developing our people."

Others spoke as well—industrial CEOs, lobbyists, journalists—and their comments, like the ones quoted above, had differences in tone and emphasis, but all struck much the same note. The future of the state depends upon the wisdom of the public policies we set today. Our best resource is our people, and we must invest in them. That means even more emphasis on education. It also means, inevitably, higher taxes to pay the bills. After a long day of businessmen, lobbyists, journalists, academics, and one novelist saying much the same thing, Cathy Mincberg asked her telling questions. "It's fine for everyone here to be in general agreement," she said, "but where are the statewide politicians who are saying these things? Who are the ones making any of this a part of their platform? Who is standing strongly for the things we've already done?"

No one had any answers. Certainly none of the handful of officeholders present leapt up to be counted, and the symposium rumbled on to the next question and the next. But the real tragedy of Texas today had been clearly exposed, though no one wanted to look directly at it. The real tragedy is not the collapse of the price of oil but our response to the collapse, especially in the political arena. If the recent primary elections proved anything, they proved that the policies that have the best chance of pulling us through an economic crisis are currently political poison. No politician running for election will advocate increasing taxes, and that's not surprising. But neither can any candidate strongly favor continuing education reform, which *is* surprising.

In the last session, the legislature passed a sweeping set of education reforms. Polls have shown that those measures are supported by a majority of Texans, but that is something you would never know from the response of teachers, administrators, and a vocal group of parents. We should not forget the reasons for the reforms: Our teachers were underpaid and overworked, and on the whole, our public schools were not doing a great job. Students were graduating with hopelessly poor skills in language and mathematics, kids were spending hours upon hours in extracurricular activities while their books gathered dust, and the contents of textbooks and classes were often sadly diluted. The reforms called for competency testing of students and teachers; the famous no pass, no play for extracurricular activities; smaller class sizes; the equalization of funding among school districts, and other measures involving discipline. Mark White lent his full support to all of those measures. And that is a major reason for his getting just over 50 percent of the vote in the Democratic primary.

Since the reforms passed, there has been little public discussion but a lot of public complaining. Teachers complain about being tested for competency. They say the test takes time and is insulting. It may take a bit of time, but it isn't insulting at all. Such tests are a way of weeding out incompetents who do nothing but perpetuate their own ignorance through their students and diminish the respect due to the large group of fine, professional teachers. Coaches and administrators complain about no pass, no play. Because many administrators were once coaches, their sympathies may be somewhat understandable. But as administrators they are responsible for building and maintaining a place of learning. That they could be against any measure that emphasizes learning over any other activity in the school is nothing short of astonishing. Yet even now the Principals Political Action Committee is gearing up to fight the reforms and probably take an active part in the governor's race. Parents have fought the no pass, no play rule in the courts and elsewhere, apparently outraged that their children might actually be required to pass courses in order to play a little ball. All this naysaying, with no one on the other side raising a voice, has produced an atmosphere of negativism. Any teacher who might favor the reforms dares not say so for fear of being ostracized from the teachers' lounge, parents dare not speak up for fear of slights from their neighbors, and politicians can't speak up for fear of being defeated at the polls. All this must end.

If the reforms need adjustment, fine. But let's do it with an attitude that assumes we're going to make them work, not one that assumes we're going to repeal them. Obviously, the governor's race is an appropriate forum for the debate of future policy, but we can only hope that this issue will be removed from the vicissitudes and demagoguery of a political campaign. If Mark White's campaign founders specifically because of his stand on education, maintaining the reforms or passing new ones will become politically impossible. Bill Clements says he's for the reforms, but he's willing to erode the provisions of no pass, no play and opposes subject-matter testing of established teachers. His position will bring many teachers and coaches into his fold. In an election year it's difficult to fault a politician for taking a politically expedient course, but such a course could be dangerous for our future. Clements should make it known that if he wins, his election would not be a victory for those who favor the coach over the classroom and who would turn the clock back on our schools. If both candidates for governor would make it quite clear that they support education reforms, the current hysteria would die down, and Texas could get on with the future.

ROY J. EATON, *Wise County Messenger*, "Wise And Otherwise" (April 24, 1986)
In the hustle and bustle of our daily lives, we are often too busy to sit back a minute and look at where we have been and where we are going.

I had the opportunity last week to attend a forum on "Texas in Transition" sponsored by the LBJ School of Public Affairs at the University of Texas in Austin and *Texas Monthly* magazine. It was well worth the effort.

Three subjects were discussed by various panel members. They were Change, Chaos and Culture; Politics and Economy; and Texas Tomorrow.

It should come as no surprise that the number one topic in each of the panel discussions was the future of agriculture and oil and gas in Texas and how the state can prosper when those two mainstays of our economy are no longer as important as they once were.

Persons from other parts of the nation have the perception that all Texans are rich oilmen or rough-hewn cowboys. That is far from the truth.

Texas is, in fact, a poor state that only once in history has reached the national average in per-capita income, and our position there was short lived.

Author Larry McMurtry, who the day before the seminar had won the Pulitzer Prize for fiction, characterized Texas as a state known for its energies that quickly turned from a rural agricultural state into an urban state.

Former UT history professor Joe B. Frantz said that occurred right after World War II when Texas was "drawn out of a rural state of mind."

A new term for my vocabulary came from Alison Cook, senior editor of *Texas Monthly*, who said Texans were deathly afraid of "Rubophobia," a word she defined as being the fear of being considered "rubes" by others.

Panelist Norman Bonner, long active in the civil rights movement, cited a number of milestones that helped bring the state's minority population into full participation as citizens.

He said Texas was spared the civil rights violence of many states because both sides used the courts instead of the streets to fight their battles.

Diana Hobby, wife of Lt. Gov. Bill Hobby, said the role of women in Texas past and present had been seriously underplayed by writers and historians. "We are known to the world by the things that men do outdoors," she said. "The best of Texas writers use women only in a periphery sense."

San Antonio Mayor Henry Cisneros told the 200 invited guests at the forum that there is no more urban state in America than Texas.

"It is a fact now that Texas has three cities in the top 10 in the nation, Dallas, Houston and San Antonio," he said. "The last time that happened was in 1865 when New York, Buffalo and Brooklyn made the list.

"The key to our future will be to educate our children and to learn to live peacefully in our cities," he said.

He cautioned Texas cities not to rely on one industry and said the future was brightest for the Dallas-Fort Worth area because of its diversified economy. "Some parts of the state are tied to Texas of the past, while other areas have tied to Texas of the future," he said.

He said he worried about the "no new taxes mentality" that is sweeping the state. "Taxes properly used are an investment," he said. "Because we want no new taxes, we are cheating our future citizens."

The domination of Texas politics by business was the topic of T. Louis Austin, president of Brown and Root, a large Texas construction firm. "It had been good for Texas," he said. "If business and government don't work together, we will be beat by our competition."

That sentiment was echoed by State Rep. Bill Messer of Belton who said the state was populated by people who believe the state offers economic opportunity.

Molly Ivins, political columnist for the *Dallas Times Herald*, disagreed. She said that business does run the legislature, which she characterized as "cheap and mean."

Scott Bennett, who grew up in Decatur and now is a columnist for the *Dallas Morning News*, was also a panelist. He said the state's business leaders have worked for the economic welfare of the state but have often not looked forward enough.

He called for an overhaul of the state's education system. "People need to know how to think, not just manage," he said. "We need to put emphasis on thinking and ideas in education."

SMU economics professor Bernard Weinstein called for more economic development in Texas. "We haven't done enough for ourselves," he said. Unlike Cisneros, Weinstein doesn't think Texas will grow much in the next 15 years.

"The oil card has been played and will not be the source of income growth for the state," Weinstein said. "We must continue to focus on upgrading of Texas's human capital."

Agriculture Commissioner Jim Hightower urged participants not to "kiss off the farmer . . . . Help them switch to more profitable crops," he said.

Paul Burka, another senior editor of *Texas Monthly*, said Texans have always had a sense of destiny, but many felt destiny is blocked by outside influence.

He also said Texans have a great belief in a good business climate. "That is the guiding principle of Texas politics. A good business climate has become sacred," he said.

After the day-long forum, which was hosted by a very gracious Lady Bird Johnson, I came away feeling several things about the future of Texas and Wise County.

First, while oil and gas and agriculture will remain very important, they aren't the only ball game in town. Tourism is already bigger than agriculture in Texas.

The sooner we begin planning our future without energy and agriculture as primary on our lists, the better off we will all be.

The second is the value of a good education system for Texas. Those at the forum were elated by the education reforms passed in Texas, and most saw an equally effective reform package around the corner for state colleges and universities.

So perhaps we should stop whining about "no pass-no play" and the 22:1 classroom requirements and some other items in the education reform package and get on with the job of making it work for all of us.

It will mean a better future for all Texans, Wise County included.

BERT HOLMES, *Dallas Times Herald*, "Investing in Texas People" (April 22, 1986)
When businessmen, economists, writers, politicians, and academicians gathered in Austin last week to talk about "Texas in transition," there was a remarkable consensus that this state is entering a new, post-oil era which demands intense cultivation of all of Texas's resources, including its people. As one panel member put it, there is not an oil-price crisis, but there is a public-policy crisis.

The Sesquicentennial forum, sponsored by the Lyndon Baines Johnson Library, the LBJ School of Public Affairs, the University of Texas at Austin and the magazine *Texas Monthly*, examined the development of Texas, its changing culture, the relationship of politics and the economy, and the challenges ahead.

In the wake of the sharp decline in oil prices, speaker after speaker said improvements in education—at all levels—will be the principal engine of future growth and progress.

Diversification was another watchword at the forum. Texas must make full use of the talents of all its people—white, black, brown and Asian, male and female—it was said again and again. It should expand its agricultural base, promote tourism, invest in research and development and expand its health-care industry, panelists urged.

San Antonio Mayor Henry Cisneros said it is time to "do something for Texas" in promoting college training for blacks and Hispanics, who will be major population groups in the decades ahead. Cultural concessions will be needed, Cisneros noted, along with a recognition that the rugged individualism of yesterday will have to change in the interest of shared opportunities.

Bernard Weinstein, an economist and the director for the Center for Enterprising at SMU, warned that the growth of Texas will slow dramatically as the state's economy adjusts to the decline in oil prices. He urged an upgrading of human capital, the improvement of the business climate through the deregulation of the finance and transportation industries, revisions in the state tax system and promotion of the entrepreneur spirit.

Bill Messer, who is leaving the Texas Legislature and his position as chairman of the finance committee of the Texas Legislature Council to become a lobbyist, said that what's good for business is good for Texas. Many of the reforms approved by the legislature—related to education, highways, water, agriculture and social programs—are business-driven, he noted. Power is decentralized, Messer pointed out, but the legislature has not succumbed to the "institutional gridlock" which has crippled Congress.

Louis Austin, former chairman of Texas Utilities and now president of Brown and Root, said he was the "fat cat spokesman" at the forum. While lamenting the disappearance of the smoke-filled room, where compromises could be developed in private, Austin urged business and government to seek practical answers to economic and environmental issues. Regulation should be reasonable, he said in complaining that there are "too many lawyers."

On the eve of primary elections, in the campaigns which have featured extensive discussions of state budgets and taxes, several panel members at the forum spoke generally of revenue enhancements. Historian Joe Frantz, for example, said it was dangerous to proclaim "no new taxes" at a time when an investment in minds is needed. And economist Weinstein said it is a myth that low taxes are good for business; other factors are more important in attracting development, including support for education.

Texans are an optimistic people, noted author Larry McMurtry, whose novel, *Lonesome Dove*, last week won the Pulitzer Prize for fiction. What the artist knows, and others should recognize, McMurtry said, is that life is not a constant upward graph. Things go in cycles, he reminded the forum. Some famous authors had successful periods and then hit a dry spell, but reached new literary heights "after going crazy."

McMurtry said Texans can handle the challenges of change without losing their minds. That's a hopeful note for a state in transition.

JAN JARBOE, *San Antonio Express-News*, "State's Future Rests in People" (April 22, 1986)
Most native Texans remember life before oil, but almost none of us can imagine a future without oil as our primary cash crop.

There was a time not so very long ago when oil was the rowdy stepchild in Texas.

Cattle and cotton were the state's first favorite sons.

I remember hearing my grandfather curse trashy oil boomers who invaded the Big Thicket in the 1930s, driving hog-raising clans and small farmers off their land.

When San Antonio financier B. K. Johnson sued his kinfolks on the King Ranch a few years ago, the most poignant moment in the trial came when a craggy-faced foreman was forced to testify that the King Ranch hadn't made money off cattle in years.

The foreman seemed humiliated that even the largest and most romantic cattle ranch in Texas eventually got hooked on oil.

The same undercurrent of anxious embarrassment was evident last week when 200 politicians, writers, academics and businessmen got together at the Lyndon Baines Johnson Library in Austin to contemplate the future of Texas.

We are the state which once had highways littered with bumper stickers proclaiming, "Freeze a Yankee in the Dark." Now, we have our collective feelings hurt over a current article in the *New Republic* magazine entitled, "Let 'Em Rot in the Sun."

"Energy is part of the DNA of our achievement," said Larry McMurtry, Pulitzer Prize-winning author of Lonesome Dove, but energy alone won't give you a considered culture."

"The legislature and Railroad Commission have managed the oil and gas industry to keep the dollars in Texas and to bring about prosperity," said Dr. David Prindle, professor of political science at the University of Texas.

"The truth is the oil industry has managed the Railroad Commission and the legislature," replied Molly Ivins, columnist for the *Dallas Times Herald*."

"The oil card has been played in Texas," said Dr. Bernard Weinstein, professor of finance at Southern Methodist University.

If Weinstein is correct, then what other cards do we have in our deck?

The consensus at the Austin forum was—as historian Dr. Joe Frantz put it—"Texas can no longer live off the bounty of the earth but must learn to live off the bounty of its people."

If that sounds like the standard pep talk Third World countries give to themselves when times are leanest, the idea of "investing in human resources" is indeed hauntingly familiar.

Perhaps the biggest secret in Texas is that we—who will sink millions in oil wells but are downright stingy about investing in education—are paralyzed by the mindset of an underdeveloped country.

Paul Burka, senior editor of *Texas Monthly* magazine, raised the central economic question—what do we have to sell? He received few specific answers.

Earlier in the day, Mayor Henry Cisneros gave his standard two-part prescription for economic and political health: diversify the economy and practice "inclusiveness" in the public arena.

The mayor ran out of time before making one of his most persuasive points—that historically cities which have prospered have been strong manufacturing centers.

Weinstein insisted the only things we'll have to sell in the future are the products of human brainpower. "If the electronics widget industry takes off in Texas, it will be because of investments in human capital," he said.

The odds of that happening seem slim to none. After all, in Texas, the word "taxes" is not a synonym for "investment," as it should be. Unfortunately, it is a synonym for political suicide.

Texas Agriculture Commissioner Jim Hightower was chock-full of ideas about futuristic products to be sold on the family farm.

He painted a vivid verbal picture of a 400-acre farm in the future that will produce special "lean cuisine" breeds of cattle stamped with a "Taste of Texas" logo and a 40-acre blueberry patch that will send its product to waiting yuppies on the East Coast.

I am straining my imagination to picture farmers—who have a difficult time amassing the necessary equipment and know-how to plant one or two staple crops every year—keeping track of the fickle yuppie market.

But maybe straining the imagination is exactly what all of us need to do to build the future—with or without oil.

SAM KINCH, Jr., *Dallas Morning News*, "Pinching Educational Pennies" (April 25, 1986)

In one sense, you could call a recent seminar here futuristic: All agreed that Texas's future depends, to a large extent, on the cultivation of the minds of our people.

The fact there was no consensus on how to go about that task is what reminds one of the Yogi Berraism, "It was *deja vu* all over again."

In just 150 years of independence from Mexico, after all, Texas has made several dramatic attempts to scale the mind-cultivation wall. All have fallen short. In every instance, the failure was due not to a lack of vision but to a lack of resource commitment.

It makes you wonder whether this self-proclaimed land of giants can finally develop itself into its own stereotype or whether we will just remain mental midgets and keep talking about it.

The "Texas in Transition" seminar at the LBJ Library on the University of Texas campus inspired that kind of bifurcated feeling: In the sesquicentennial of our history, can Texans overcome their pride in a niggardly view of human-resource development? Or will we remain content with being first in myth writers' material but among the last in education and social services and amenities?

It is not an idle set of questions. As oil peters out—just as cotton did before, and open-range ranching did before that—what is Texas's replacement commodity? We're just about out of natural resources to exploit, so logic and history suggest our human resource is next on the development agenda.

But that is a long road. For years, in the name of "a good bidness climate" and of "no new taxes," we have consigned the underclasses to perpetual intellectual poverty, the middle classes to mediocrity and the upper classes to whatever they can afford.

We have cheated ourselves on the quality of education, from the first grade to the last (which typically, has been about the 10th—we also come close to leading the nation in dropouts). We have imposed on our universities a conformity of curriculum as well as a need to compete like hungry dogs for the available state money.

We have concluded that research is a waste of time unless it expands a payroll. And we have regarded many of the co-curricular activities, notably the fine arts, as sissified.

Football has in some ways become the Texas paradigm. Less than 5 per cent of the population play the game, typically, but in small towns it is still the predominant folkway and for some, football is still the only thing of which a state college can be truly proud.

In our view of ourselves, we haven't done much better. The dominant Anglo (since the bloody revolution against Mexico in 1836, at least) hasn't had many positive thoughts about his fellow Texans of color: Blacks were brought in as slaves, for the most part, and were never encouraged to be much more than sharecroppers.

And Mexican-Americans, whose Texas ancestors predated all but a few Anglos, have long been regarded as not much more than a source of cheap labor. (Academic literature is replete with evidence that poor whites also have been treated on the human scale as mere units of labor; as with the Indians, however, Texans have chosen politically to ignore this particular chapter of the Texas textbook.)

For the future, though, all that will have to change. By the early 2000s, black and brown and yellow Texans will be a majority in the schools, and not long thereafter a voting majority. So we in the current majority have more than just our racial and ethnic attitudes to alter.

The fact is, until we all sit at the same table in terms of educational and survival services, we can't really talk about a Texas future. And we can't get to the same table until we make a state commitment that a) there will be chairs for all, even if that requires extra help for some, and b) the same basic educational plate will be available to all, with follow-up education an option based on talent.

All this will cost money. But it's also true that the Texas business community is ready to pay more in taxes for programs that enrich or ennoble the state's people and that carry at least a fair potential for making us more than what we are today.

Indeed, the most farsighted businessmen realize that not only do we need an educated work force to handle today's job needs, we need employable people who also are smart enough and retrainable enough to change careers one or more times after they enter the marketplace.

Come to think of it, that wouldn't be a bad mind-cultivation goal. It's also not a bad summation of the UT seminar: To have a future, we must change and we must do so in a way that includes all of us educationally, culturally, economically and politically.

ANNA MACIAS, *Dallas Morning News*, "Texans Look Toward Future" (April 19, 1986)

It is time for Texans to recognize their achievements, dispel the myths about their state and plan for their future, a panel asserted Friday at a symposium titled "Texas in Transition: A Sesquicentennial Forum."

Panelists included San Antonio Mayor Henry Cisneros, *Texas Monthly* senior editor Alison Cook, Pulitzer Prize-winning author Larry McMurtry, University of Texas law professor Norman Bonner and Diana Hobby, wife of Lieutenant Governor Bill Hobby. Joe Frantz, a history professor at Corpus Christi State University, moderated the discussion, held at the Lyndon Baines Johnson Library on the University of Texas campus.

Lady Bird Johnson, University of Texas president Bill Cunningham and U.S. Rep. Jake Pickle, D-Texas, also attended the forum.

The panel discussed change, chaos and culture in Texas's past, present and future.

The myths are well known, Frantz said. "Everyone knows there are 49 states, and Texas is just an affiliate. Everyone thinks we're all funny. We're all yah-hoos.

"But here we are a people who would like to be recognized. We have something to be proud of," he said.

"What has distinguished Texas is its industries. Not its oil industries, but its human industries," McMurtry said. "Sheer, raw energy is a central part of achievement."

Ms. Cook said the oil industry historically was important in the state's growth. "That black stuff has fueled tremendous changes in Texas," she said. "It gave us our cities. Oil booted Texas into an auto culture. Oil and gas taxes gave us our road system . . . that bound us all together."

The panelists agreed that the state is too economically dependent on the oil industry and must strengthen its educational system.

Contrary to popular views of Texas, Cisneros said, "There isn't a more urban state in America. There isn't another state that has 28 urban areas within its boundaries." Houston, Dallas and San Antonio are among the nation's 10 largest cities, Cisneros said.

Texans haven't really faced the question of whether they really value the bounty of their people, Cisneros said.

"Texas was able to build off of the bounty of the earth. We were fortunate," he said. "Mother Nature put oil under the ground and made the water and the topography hospitable to cattle.

"California, on the other hand, has relied on the bounty of its people, building a great university system, and as a result, has prepared itself for the next economy," Cisneros said.

"If it were a nation, California would be the sixth most powerful nation in the world," he said. "They have the greatest aggregation of technological knowledge in the world in one physical place."

Frantz said improving the state's schools was essential regardless of the cost.

"Taxes properly used are an investment," Frantz said. "We need to invest in the minds of our youth. We need to get them trained . . . let them have insights."

The Lyndon Baines Johnson Library has hosted 20 similar panel discussions since 1972, according to Max Sherman, dean of the Lyndon B. Johnson School of Public Affairs.

The sesquicentennial theme of the discussion was a way

to extend the dialogue started in the January sesquicentennial issue of *Texas Monthly*, said forum organizer Michael Gillette.

There is lots of room for improvement in the state, the panelists concurred.

"The history of Texas will persist," Ms. Cook said. "Nothing has been decided yet.

"The world hasn't been finished yet."

GEOFFREY RIPS, *Texas Observer*, "Texas in Transition" (May 16, 1986)

"Our presence here is all vain glory;
This false world is but transitory."

William Dunbar, 1465–1530

While the Dallas councilwoman lunched on barbecue with the public relations executive from Austin, the economist from Southern Methodist University, and the printer and political leader from San Antonio in the basement of the LBJ Library, 182 university students, teachers, and community members were being arrested on the university's west mall. While the Brown & Root executive discussed gummint and bidness with two state legislators, a journalist, and an academic in the house that Brown & Root helped build, students were calling the investment policy of the state institution into question. While the San Antonio mayor discussed the oil bust and opening economic corridors in a room from which all natural light was excluded via cardboard taped over windows and skylights for the benefit of video cameras, the smoke surrounding the bombing of Libya had not yet cleared.

Oh, the oil bidness! the oil bidness! How they quake and moan when it ain't going good. San Antonio Mayor Henry Cisneros, for instance, managed to reduce the great rhetorical sweep you expect from a politician to a rather humble vision by running together a few cliches: "We like to think of ourselves," he told the audience, "as . . . masters of our destiny over everything we see within our reach." Though it would not be his point until a few sentences later, Cisneros had inadvertently shrunk our future to that which is already within our grasp. That's not the way they used to think in *Giant*.

But these leaders and thinkers and reporters were brought together on April 18 by the LBJ Library and *Texas Monthly* to discuss Texas in transition. And the transition they were feeling most keenly was from the four decades of devil-may-care, laissez faire oil prosperity to the darkly lit corridors of what may not be as propitious a future.

It was billed as a sesquicentennial forum. But as historian and moderator Joe Frantz pointed out, the 150 year demarcation is a formulation that ignores "the fact that we go back 458 years." And had there been any Native Americans among us, that formulation, too, would have seemed myopic. To this, Diana Hobby added that the history of Texas has been written as a history of "the things that men do outdoors."

This was echoed at a later panel by a recent history of what men do indoors—in the halls of the state capitol—as rendered by state representative Bill Messer of Belton and seconded by T. Louis Austin, chief executive of Brown & Root, and political consultant George Christian, who said Texas was blessed with "a dazzling display of leadership after World War II." Messer, who doubles as a lobbyist for tort reform and trucking interests until his term ends this year, espoused a philosophy for which his legislative service provides living testimony. "Texas," Messer, said, "is populated by citizens who believe Texas offers economic opportunity. That's why they elect [those concerned with bidness] to the legislature and not social engineers. For three or four decades we had a conservative political and bidness establishment that worked together, hand in glove—basically scandal-free—and did what Texans wanted done. Gummint tended to the bidness of bidness."

Now Mr. Messer subscribes to a peculiar reading of history, a history in which Jerry Sadler and Gus Mutscher, among others, apparently never took part. It is a peculiar reading, but one, nonetheless, subscribed to by most of those in the bidness of gummint, who believe, along with Messer, that what's good for bidness is good for Texas. T. Louis Austin, who ran Texas Utilities before joining Brown & Root, chimed in: "We've over-democratized this country so that we no longer have smoke-filled rooms. You can't run a good democracy without a smoke-filled room."

All this democracy, coupled with an economic downturn, has knocked these fellas for a loop. Bill Messer blamed this democracy business on the change to single-member districts in the early 1970s, followed by the application of the Voting Rights Act to Texas in 1975. But despite the relative diversity this has brought to Texas politics, Messer averred, "Texas is still a very homogeneous state. They [Texans] agree on 90 per cent of what gummint is doing. All this is good for bidness." But now, without the oil prosperity to support such egalitarian measures as indigent health care demanded by the rabble, how is the state to manage all this democracy? ("More likely it will remain the only industrial state without an income tax," George Christian offered, more as a statement of will than analysis.)

David Prindle, author of a book on the Railroad Commission, said Texas is currently suffering from a management problem. "We don't have an oil price crisis in Texas," he said. "We have a public-policy crisis." SMU finance professor Bernard Weinstein said economic development was the key, adding that "we are an over-regulated state," in which entrepreneurship must be encouraged. Which brings us to Mayor Cisneros's major contribution to the debate: a reading, complete with explication, of Robert Frost's "The Road Not Taken." But in Cisneros's version, the desolate path is more a multi-lane corridor connecting Dallas to Austin to San Antonio, upon which the Mack trucks of economic diversification flatten the poets of isolation and reflection.

But is that Texas in transition—moving from an economy based on oil and cheap labor to one based on oil, real estate, high technology, and cheap labor? In this forum dedicated to trickle-down social policy, economic development and diversification were largely the elements of transition. But not outside. Had the cardboard been removed from the windows and the doors removed from their jambs, then Texas in flux might have been better understood.

The forum participants were given a glimpse of that real world by economist Wilbur Cohen, who, from the audience, said that in ten years the state's population would be older and more diverse, its needs greater and the necessity to answer those needs more urgent. Earl Lewis of Trinity University and the Select Committee on Higher Education said the real transition would be toward a "quality of life available to the generality of the people." We must, he said, "abandon our faithfulness to a tradition that provides inadequate human and health-care services. Those currently and historically underserved by our institutions will be more than 50 per cent of the Texans under 15 in the year 2000." Lewis urged a new understanding of the fact that public welfare serves the wealthy and middle class and not the poor, that government is not the problem, and that "we must lose some respect for the sanctity and purity of market forces." Did the cardboard come unglued to allow this light in? Not many noticed.

There is movement in this state. Bill Messer and conservative columnist Scott Bennett sense it, as they uncharacteristically called for gummint to take a larger role in managing economic affairs. Lieutenant Governor Bill Hobby, of all the legislative officials, probably best understands it, as he marshalls the forces of change to the extent that his sense of *noblesse oblige* will allow.

The last ten years of oil boom and bust, the last forty years of oil prosperity, the last 150 years of statehood are points too small to be isolated and, in that way, measured. In order to understand the changes in the life of this state, they must be understood in the context of the larger world. Mass migration from Mexico may still be part of the process equalizing the resources stolen from that republic one and a half centuries ago. The migration from Central America is certainly the equal and opposite reaction to the actions of our country's foreign and economic policy in that region. The economy of Fort Worth depends on the weapons sold to fortify the Middle East. Until the world at large and the Texans of the next fifty years enter the conversation, as they inevitably will, our public policy-makers will flounder, and the economy of the state will be blown back and forth by winds we will not be able to forecast or understand.

BOB ROGERS, *Bryan-College Station Eagle,* "Coming to Terms with Texas's Future" (April 27, 1986)
Texas, he said, is like a youngster with an inheritance. It grew up attractive and somewhat troublesome, without having to think. When the range cattle ran out, it got another inheritance, this one called Spindletop. Rich with oil, the youngster forged ahead, still attractive, still troublesome, still not thinking.

Today, the second inheritance also has dwindled, and suddenly the attractive, troublesome youngster for the first time faces the necessity of having to think.

Historian Joe B. Frantz thus characterized the theme of "Texas in Transition," a Sesquicentennial forum sponsored by the Lyndon B. Johnson Library and the LBJ School of Public Affairs.

Most of the participants described a future that must break with the past. They talked about diversification, education, and high technology. They foresaw a new kind of population with important implications for education and politics. They urged divestiture of some favorite myths as a necessity for coping with new realities.

The oil industry is not dead, they agreed, but its dominance of the state's life almost certainly is.

"The oil card," said SMU economist Bernard Weinstein, "has been played." Others predicted that the price of oil surely will rise again, but no matter, Weinstein said, the oil economy is over, and because it is we must look to people who can read, write, compute and analyze.

That is one of the challenges to education, but the schools also must understand the implications of a changing population. Among Texans under the age of 15, the majority already is black and brown.

San Antonio Mayor Henry Cisneros, a member of the Texas A&M University board of regents, suggested that education has not yet come to grips with that new reality. At A&M, he said, only 4 per cent of the students are Hispanic, although Hispanics already represent 17 per cent of the state's population. And only 3 per cent at A&M are blacks, though they make up 15 per cent of the population.

If, Cisneros warned, we do not adequately serve this increasing segment of our people, we may one day see a legislature dominated by people who are angry and frustrated because the sytem never really worked for them.

Norman Bonner, an Austin lawyer sitting in for State Senator Craig Washington, joined with Cisneros in calling for a "politics of inclusion." That kind of politics, Cisneros said, can happen only by effort and through structures, a delicate way of saying that governments and public institutions will have to act to make it happen.

Larry McMurtry, who had been awarded the Pulitzer Prize for his novel *Lonesome Dove* only two days before the forum, also noted the need for deliberate approaches. Societies, he said, are not necessarily progressive. They have to learn new skills. They have to think and plan.

McMurtry also expressed hope that Texas in transition would move from its first phase, a culture of survival, to a more enlightened one that will stress development of the imagination.

Several speakers disputed the validity of some widely held Texas tenets.

Weinstein: Keeping taxes low and the unions out to encourage business simply "doesn't play." In reality, he said, we must be willing to keep up services and to pay for them.

Weinstein: Texas is not an entrepreneurial state. In the last three years the number of new businesses in Texas went down, while the number in California and Massachusetts increased rapidly.

Frantz: Taxes properly used are an investment in the future. The no-new-taxes shibboleth is the most dangerous element in our current politics.

Cisneros: Unbridled individualism no longer will work. Instead, we must have cooperation and a measure of consensus.

Paul Burka, a senior editor at *Texas Monthly* magazine, provided a kind of valedictory to the day with a recitation of factors that he said govern Texas life and politics.

For one thing, he said, Texas is a poor state, consistently below the national average in income, its mythological riches notwithstanding.

For another, Texans have a sense of destiny that provides useful optimism but also can be perverse, leading to anti-elitism, lack of sophistication, and isolation.

And finally, there is the state's traditional xenophobia, which creates suspicions of everything non-Texan. Burka recalled the quintessential xenophobe, Governor Jim Ferguson, who objected to the teaching of foreign languages in Texas schools with this definitive argument:

If, Ferguson said, English was good enough for Jesus, it was good enough for the schoolchildren of Texas.

MARK SINGER, *The New Yorker* (May 19, 1986)
A friend writes:

The other day, I flew to Texas, and on the last leg of my trip, from Dallas to Austin, one of the flight attendants committed the error, more than once, of announcing our destination as Houston. This offended some of my fellow-passengers—caused a couple of them to yelp in distress. Texas is many different places, and local chauvinism is a basic industry throughout the state. The year 1986 is the year of Texas's hundred-and-fiftieth birthday—its sesquicentennial. The earnest celebrating began several months ago, but the fervor has subsided as certain new facts of life in Texas have become more vivid. Houston, for instance, which for decades boomed and sprawled without much thought given to the negative potential of boom and sprawl, is now experiencing severe hardships and permanent readjustments—consequences of the gradual decline and then the sudden collapse of the price of crude oil. My specific reason for going to Texas was to listen to several interesting thinkers meditate aloud during an event called Texas in Transition: A Sesquicentennial Forum. This daylong discussion, which one participant—Jim Hightower, the Texas Commissioner of Agriculture—described as "this sesquicentennial dialogue and high-level hog-calling contest," took place on the eighth floor of the Lyndon Baines Johnson Library and Museum, in a red-carpeted atrium that had potted schefflera and ficus trees, television cameras and bright lights, and seating for two hundred and fifty people.

The transition that Texas is going through is the transition from mythology to a not terribly comforting reality. Henry Cisneros, the Mayor of San Antonio, who participated in a panel discussion of "Change, Chaos and Culture," pointed out that the critical public issues that Texas must address in the near future "will no longer be the problems of the range but they will be the problems of how we build highways and schools and educate our people and live together in the cities of our state." Movies and television and books have given the world images of Texas that are, of course, limited in their scope. Instead of thinking of Texas as it actually exists—an urban state (it has three of the ten most populous cities in the country, and fifteen years from now only California will have more people) and a not altogether prosperous state (it has a per capita income below the national average and a larger poverty population than New York State's, and fifteen years from now half the young people in Texas will be black or Hispanic)—most non-Texans, when they hear the word "Texas," conjure up the brash vulgarity of Jett Rink in "Giant" or the sinister rapacity of a J. R. Ewing or an H. L. Hunt or the folklore that has come to us from J. Frank Dobie. For a number of reasons, it has been more convenient to consider Texas in these terms than to consider a Texas with the diversity, pluralism, and spiritual amplitude of, say, New York City. Europeans, it seems, have customarily imagined Texas to be a magnified metaphor for America. One irony of this particular myth is that the Texas sesquicentennial commemorates not the beginning of statehood but the founding of the Republic of Texas, which fought for and won independence from Mexico. Or, as one participant in the sesquicentennial forum observed, "Texas is not really a member of the United States but an affiliate."

There were three panel discussions, and the panelists included twenty or so writers, educators, and public officials (like Jim Hightower and Henry Cisneros). A theme that echoed throughout the day was that Texas has been blessed with a prodigious natural inheritance—hydrocarbons, and also arable and grazeable land—but that the uncertain value of this inheritance (the only certainty being that the value has declined) now requires the citizens of Texas to examine their self-worth. Texas, one speaker said, "has to decide to decide" on the answers to some of the questions that confront it. "Texas has been able to build off the bounty of the earth," said Mayor Cisneros. "California, on the other hand, in the last forty years or so, anyway, has relied on the bounty of its people. . . . I don't think we're prepared to invest in our people yet. We haven't really crossed over the threshold of some very critical decisions about whether we really value all our people in Texas."

The novelist Larry McMurtry, who had just been announced as the winner of the Pulitzer Prize in Fiction for his novel *Lonesome Dove,* was another participant in the discussion of "Change, Chaos and Culture." "We are one of the most optimistic states in an optimistic nation," McMurtry said. "There have been so many givens in this state. There is so much here that essentially only had to be used and exploited—that didn't have to be planned, particularly." Such chronic optimism, he continued, has drawbacks. Does winning a Pulitzer Prize this year mean that he is duty-bound to win it again next year and the year after? And if he fails to win public prizes should he then decide to switch careers? "Texas does have to come to grips with the basic psychological fact that societies are not necessarily and inevitably progressive—that things don't always get better and better."

And so the high-level hog-calling proceeded. There was barbecue for lunch and a Tex-Mex buffet in the evening—reminders that the native spirits of both Lyndon Johnson and Antonio Lopez de Santa Anna were present for the occasion. One of the afternoon panelists, an economist from Dallas, read excerpts from unsympathetic out-of-state editorials that have appeared recently about the decline of oil prices and its effect upon Texas. A lot of non-Texas money found its way into Texas pockets during the late seventies and early eighties, with the dramatic rise of petroleum and everything that depended upon it. This happened for a multitude of reasons, but among them was not that a Texas cabal had seized control of the planet. The money also found its way into many pockets outside Texas. During the energy crisis, a popular bumper sticker that could be seen in Texas and other energy-producing states said, "Let the Yankee Bastards Freeze in the Dark." And, now that the world has turned, there has emerged a corollary sentiment, which, expressed in bumper-stickerese, says, "Let Texas Rot in the Sun." Meanwhile, every month, tens of thousands of refugees—seeking, like Texas's own original colonists, not religious or intellectual freedom but economic betterment—leave their homes in Mexico and Central America and wind up in what may geographically be Texas but, more significantly, is the United States. If Texas does rot in the sun, it is not Jett Rink and J. R. Ewing and H. L. Hunt who will suffer.

The afternoon session at the LBJ Library dragged on rather too long, it felt at moments, but that was because it had evolved into a town meeting, characterized by spontaneity, bombast, imaginativeness, pomposity, posturing, heartfelt self-expression—the gamut. One frequently uttered thought was that Texas might ultimately find a way out of its present mess if the state would devote extraordinary resources over the next few decades to educating its young citizens—an expensive undertaking—and this led to brave and honest calls for Texans to outgrow their unwillingness to tax themselves. (In Texas, at the moment, there are no personal or corporate income taxes.) One member of the audience proposed that Texas would be a whole lot better off if it had fewer traffic lights. There were eloquent statements and unintelligible non sequiturs—in other words, all the rewards and burdens of pure democracy. Finally, Ronnie Dugger, the writer and editor who in 1954 helped to found *The Texas Observer*, rose and made plain that the topic of the day—Texas in Transition—was, above all, not a local matter.

"There is much that is serious, valuable, and worthwhile, but there can also be something almost quaint, in our meeting here like this talking about Texas in transition, when the overriding question for any of us, Texans or Polynesians, is whether there will be anything to transition to," Ronnie Dugger said. "If we could simply choose what transition to be in, I would choose that—while preserving and celebrating our uniqueness as a state and working together on our present chances and problems—we stop thinking of ourselves as if our Texas borders in any way protected us from television, refugees, hungry and unemployed Mexican workers, revolutions, tourists, terrorists, domestic monopolies, the international oil cartel, wars in Lebanon or Angola or Nicaragua, or missiles in Russia. Texans, we are Americans. Americans, we are human beings. That is the real transition that is happening, and should be."

So much, therefore for the belief, wherever it persists, that there is nothing wrong with Texas that a twenty-five-dollar-per-barrel rebound in the price of oil (and maybe a fivefold rise in the prices of wheat and cotton and sorghum) would not repair. Evidently, Texas, a hundred and fifty years after establishing its independence, has joined the real world.

KYLE THOMPSON, *Fort Worth Star-Telegram*, "Ro(i)lling Along" (April 27, 1986)

The uniqueness of Texas and the 16 million people who call it their home state is evidenced by the fact that even with oil prices falling to the modern-day unheard of price of $12 a barrel, we still can find room for optimism.

This appeared to be the overriding theme at a recent symposium entitled "Texas in Transition: A Sesquicentennial Forum". Panelists at the day-long session at the LBJ Library on the University of Texas at Austin campus ranged from the erudite San Antonio Mayor Henry Cisneros to Pulitzer Prize-winning author Larry McMurtry to politicians to university scholars.

Among the several dozen guests were a cross section of the state's top news executives, educators and business executives. They were invited to take an intensive look at how we Texans arrived at where we are today and at what is likely to happen to us and to our state in the near future.

What seemed to thread its way through the discussions was the assertion that in the half century since Texas celebrated its centennial in 1936, we have just about completed the transition from a rural to an urban society and no longer can rely on oil as the basis of our economic and political structure.

Another consensus was that Texans now and in the future must rely more and more on human resources rather than on natural resources.

McMurtry, named winner of the Pulitzer Prize for his latest novel, *Lonesome Dove*, the day before the conference, summed up this theme when he said that "what distinguishes Texas is its industries. Not its oil industries, but its human industries. Sheer, raw energy is a central part of achievement."

Economists, educators and political leaders told the conference that the Texas myth that self-reliance and a frontier economy can meet the needs of the people will not pull the state out of its economic and social slide. Texas, they concluded, is in the throes of rapid changes.

"Texas is at a juncture and faces some difficult choices," said Cisneros. "Parts of our state are hitched totally to an economy of the past—oil and agriculture. Other sections, like the Dallas-Fort Worth area, are more dynamic because they chose to diversify some time ago. Now, all of us need to travel down the road of consensus. Texas has been able to build off the bounty of the earth, but others, such as Californians, relied on the bounty of their people.

"What we in Texas must do is invest in the bounty of our people. I don't think we are yet ready to do that, but our future lies in the education of our people—all of our people, whether they be white, black or brown. Our future lies in the politics of inclusion. We must embrace all segments of the population. Texas now is at a point where we are not necessarily going to continue progressing. We are going to have to think and to try new innovations," Cisneros said.

The two dozen or more panelists agreed as one on the topic of education as an essential element in the future of Texas. Trinity University professor Earl Lewis pointed out that by the year 2000 more than 50 per cent of the Texans under 15 years of age will be Hispanic or black. "It will be a challenge for us to get geared up to provide development of that large a contingent of people. Education is going to be essential to get all of us to the table of rewards and prosperity."

There were some pessimists. Dr. Bernard Weinstein of Dallas said the economic outlook for Texas over the next 15 years is one of slowed growth and a sharp drop in people moving into the state.

Part of the problem, the SMU economist said, is due to the fact that Texas occupied itself with the oil and gas boom of the 1970's and ignored the need for economic development in other areas. "The oil card has been played," he said. "Oil is not going to be a source of income and employment growth in the future in Texas."

But University of Texas political science professor David Prindle said the state doesn't need natural resources to be prosperous. States in the Northeast have no natural resources—they rely on education "and an effective way of collecting taxes." Prindle noted that Texas is the only large industrial state without a state income tax.

Other speakers pointed out that despite its reputation, Texas is a poor state. One speaker noted that the only time Texans reached the national per capita personal income was during the oil boom of the 1970s.

In all the speeches and discussions, the subject always seemed to focus on education as the main ingredient of a successful future for Texas. And that, in the final analysis, was the most important conclusion of the gathering.

William Broyles, Jr., a journalist who recently returned to Texas after working out of state for six years, said the single biggest change he had noted was a change in the attitude toward education.

"Texas is on the right track in public school reform," Broyles said. "We Texans always had frontier faith. We believed if we got up early and worked hard, we would succeed. Now, more and more of us find this is not necessarily true. What we now must concentrate on is the development of our human resources. This will determine the real future of Texas."

Success will come to modern-day Texans, then, if we get up early, work hard and educate ourselves. The myths of self-reliance and a frontier economy no longer are enough.

BILL WALRAVEN, *Corpus Christi Caller*, "Experts Gather to Mull Future of Texas" (April 22, 1986)

State Agriculture Commissioner Jim Hightower called it "a high-level hog-calling contest."

It was A Sesquicentennial Forum at the Lyndon B. Johnson School of Public Affairs in Austin which included some pretty gaudy names, including Pulitizer Prize winner Larry McMurtry, San Antonio Mayor Henry Cisneros and other writers, editors, businessmen, historians, professors and politicians.

The full day of talk sponsored by the LBJ Library and Museum, the LBJ School of Public Affairs, the University of Texas and *Texas Monthly* magazine, was entitled "Texas in Transition," and generally here are some of the ideas I picked up before my mind became totally gridlocked:

Texas is in a heap of economic trouble and can't expect much help from Yankees who are now saying "Let 'em rot in the sun."

Texas rode the comet of Arab oil prices and relied so heavily on its riches that the 1970s were an "aberration."

Even if $25 oil returns, it will never regain its former importance and henceforth will remain merely a commodity.

Texas has concentrated on growth instead of development and became overly dependent on oil in East and West Texas, too heavily dependent on agriculture in other sections and too heavily dependent on the Mexican peso along the border.

The answer in each instance is diversification.

Strangely, tourism, which helps give this area a diverse economy along with oil, agriculture and the military, was scarcely mentioned.

The general solution to the problem is education. California invested in education early and has reaped human profits whereas Texas "won the lottery" and has lived off government land, oil and the largess of the Earth.

Minority spokesmen argued for literacy of the masses to support an urban society while the academicians called for excellence in higher education, saying only one Texas university division has been declared the best in the nation.

Some predicted the state's population will be 20 million by the year 2000. Another said the immigration from other states will reach Ground Zero in 1986 from a high of 300,000 a year and will cease being a factor in growth.

Texas, unless it solves its urban mass transit problems, will have complete freeway gridlock in the major cities.

By 1990, Texas will have three of the top 10 cities: Houston, Dallas and San Antonio.

By the year 2000, half the Texas population under the age of 15 will be black, brown or yellow.

Texas is a poor state and will continue to be. Houston has more poor than the entire population of Newark, N.J.

Thirty per cent of the schoolchildren of Texas never get beyond the ninth grade. Some 65 per cent of the people do not read at all even though they may be literate.

Conservatives claimed Texas business is overregulated. Liberals countered that businessmen come to Austin begging to be regulated.

For the future, dryland farming will have to change, making use of slurry water and reclaimed salt water. Farmers will diversify to cattle, catfish, oriental vegetables, herbs, grapes and Christmas trees and will sell directly to markets.

"Cutting the fat" in higher education threatens to drive out talented professors. Community colleges will increase in importance in educating displaced workers.

Texas will face a crisis in education and human needs at a time when a burgeoning elderly population will vote against financing.

A number of times it was suggested that with Texas's pay-as-you-go budget, a state income and possibly a state industrial tax will become necessary.

Folklorist John Henry Faulk said ignorance is no hindrance to membership in the Texas Legislature and Cisneros jolted me with this information: "The year 2000 is only 14 years away. What were you doing in 1972? That was 14 years ago."

That worried me more than all the oil in Saudi Arabia..

CHARLES WORTH WARD, *Wichita Falls Times*, "A Future for Texas: Will the Stars Shine Bright for the State Another 100 Years?" (May 18, 1986)

> Among my earliest memories is being held in my father's arms and seeing lots of feather fans and balloons. I was about 3. I later realized that mind's eye picture was from Billy Rose's Show that ushered in the 1936 Texas Centennial.
>
> This was about 50 years ago, about the time my late father lost all the family cotton gins. Cotton was

plowed under to save the market for the hundreds of farmers the Ward gins served in Central Texas.

The family moved to Wichita Falls and Dad found a living in oil. He had to work all his life to financially rebound. But when he died 20 years ago he owned the largest crude oil brokerage firm in this area. All my life I've benefitted directly or indirectly from black gold. Now that I'm 50 and the area's major economic resource is in trouble, I wonder about the future.

My grandparents saw the fading of the cattle frontier as my parents witnessed the fall of "King Cotton." What of the next 50 years until Texas's 200th birthday?

By Charles Worth Ward

Everything is going to be all right in Texas, at least early in the next century. This was the consensus reached by Texas leaders gathered at the LBJ Library to assess "Texas in Transition" during its Sesquicentennial.

With the oil price crisis playing havoc with the state's economic base and fading agriculture, leaders are seeking a new economic dynamic. Better education appears to be a big part of the answer.

Henry Cisneros, mayor of San Antonio, warned of the masses of unemployed along the Rio Grande and the likelihood that unrest in Mexico will bring more immigrants into Texas. Cisneros pointed out that border areas of Texas are in trouble, with oil- and land-based industries fading. He said even the heart of Texas (Dallas-Fort Worth, Waco-Austin and Bryan-College Station) will feel bad economic times.

Texas is a long way from the "friendly Indians" from which its name is derived. By the turn of the century the state will be home to almost twenty million souls. That means the state, which took 150 years to reach 15 million, will have grown by another third and will have 28 metropolitan areas.

Diana Hobby, wife of Lieutenant Governor Bill Hobby, said early day Texas appealed to the macho in men "because it sanctioned violence." She said this manifests itself today in our high interest in sports. Mrs. Hobby, a longtime book editor, praised John Graves's *Goodbye to a River* and the work of Dan Jenkins, both of Fort Worth. But her highest praise went to Larry McMurtry's *In a Narrow Grave* for its insight into the state's early days.

McMurtry is from Archer City, Texas. His book tells of the settling of the frontier from here to the Panhandle.

It's not as if McMurtry, who spoke at the seminar, hasn't done other fine work. Many North Texans think *Lonesome Dove,* his epic of early day cattle drives, is his best. It earned the Pulitzer Prize for fiction.

McMurtry said that at age 50 he has witnessed during his lifetime the transition in Texas from rural to urban. He warned of the traffic gridlock that threatens the state's urban areas and praised the human "energy" he saw on a recent tour of small colleges in Texas.

"We are one step from the frontier. Concern is with the survival of our culture, families, and economics. General education reforms will bring us closer to a better Texas," he said.

Alison Cook, senior editor of *Texas Monthly,* one of the sponsors of the event, said "Nothing has been decided in Texas as yet." She said the latest boom in oil helped bring in people from all over the world. Many will stay, and thus change the state.

Joe Frantz, Texas historian, said we must face this change in our population mix and do as California did in upgrading education, planning and setting goals. Indeed, "diversify" and "educate" were the two themes that kept coming up during the seminar.

How? Where to find the money? These questions are hard to answer.

Suggestions ranged from proposals for a state income tax and putting more taxes on business to older solutions. Horses, dogs and lotteries all might be tapped. The trouble is, even in a state that has all but done away with prohibition of alcohol, mores are such that the public has refused to support gambling.

It is doubtful sin taxes can fill state coffers depleted of oil taxes.

Meg Wilson, Governor Mark White's economic development expert, spoke of "the pain of transition" as Texas lays plans to diversify.

Dr. Earl Lewis, a Trinity University urban expert, pointed to the disparity of income for non-whites and warned that "by the year 2000 more than half of the state's population under 15 will be non-white. Better get ready," he warned. "In 1979, 14.7 per cent of Texas's population was at the poverty level. Surpluses exist, but the poverty level is holding."

Texas Monthly's political pundit warned of Texas banks being controlled from elsewhere. There seemed to be a fear of New York taking control of Texas institutions. Perhaps Texas has a complex about the East. It says a great deal about the nature of Texans that they even think it is possible to keep the economic ball from New York.

Bill Broyles, founding editor of *Texas Monthly*, discussed his return to Houston after editing stops in California and as editor of *Newsweek*.

How does this discussion relate to Wichita Falls and the Red River? Not mentioned was the importance of the Dallas-Fort Worth International Airport, development of a world market center in Dallas or Fort Worth's art leadership. Houston as a world class health center was alluded to, as was the made-in-Texas movie boom. Tourism was touted as Texas's second largest industry.

All these areas can be developed to at least some extent in Wichita Falls, but we must plan for the future. Wichitans hate to see their offspring have to go to the larger cities to work. Wichita Falls is not suffering the unemployment jump as are other cities of its size. We have water, rainfall, an expanding economic base and an intense interest in our future. A cadre of young adults is attaining real power, hospitals are expanding, more financial institutions are being born and talk of a better, more beautiful city abounds.

If we plan, fund, educate and diversify, can we hope for better times ahead?

Perhaps so, but there is no panacea. One theme was that we must learn to plan as well as place more economic resources in human needs, since the state is among the lowest in expenditures for education and social services.

The jury is out on whether the Texas spirit will prevail if not funded by the earth's bounty.

Other observations include the surprise that former U.S. Senator John Tower, the person many felt rekindled the Republican Party in the South, was referred to only in passing, and credit for the party buildup was all given to former Governor Bill Clements. After watching and covering Tower for about a quarter of a century, I know Tower had a profound effect in Texas politics.

George Christian, who along with Liz Carpenter are sort of semi-official window keepers into the Johnson years, spoke of the old FDR populism mixture with rock bed capitalism, a mix that of late is not much in vogue.

In a state where Academy Award-winning movies were made this year; a fiction writer and the *Dallas Morning News* won top prizes in literature; Dr. Denton Cooley continues leadership in the health revolution; Dallas is the national mercantile leader; entrepreneurs in Houston are planning the world's largest airline; Vice President George Bush is the early front-runner for the GOP presidential bid; Phil Gramm is laying a national political base; and the Democrats are looking to Mark White and Commissioner of Agriculture Jim Hightower for leadership nationally; and Henry Cisneros need choose only when, where and what leadership role he will exercise, it is difficult to write off Texas.

H. Ross Perot was famous for computer leadership before he became involved in education reforms; Dallas is emerging as a leader in the dance scene; the Austin sound continues to be big; and imagination and intuition abound. Believing all this is going to disappear is impossible.

Perhaps we might stop our self-torture, forget who we were and where we are and think about where we're going.

But Texas fail? Never.

FELTON WEST, *Houston Post*, "Texans Hold a Meeting of Minds" (April 27, 1986)

> Why has the Texas Legislature been so partial to business?
>
> How does a liberal describe the Legislature?
>
> Why has the Republican Party grown so fast in Texas recently?

There was a lot of thought-provoking commentary on these and many other subjects in Austin recently at a Sesquicentennial forum called Texas in Transition. Sponsored by the Lyndon Baines Johnson Library, the LBJ School of Public Affairs at the University of Texas and *Texas Monthly* magazine, the meeting at the presidential library presented 21 panelists for a full day of discussions on "The Making of Modern Texas" and "Texas Tomorrow."

For listeners, the forum's arrangers drew together about 240 people, including writers, historians, educators, politicians, bureaucrats and news media representatives.

Discussing the state's development, Alison Cook, a *Texas Monthly* senior editor, said Texas is "still in the process of inventing itself" and still has the pervasive feeling that "nothing has been decided yet."

Panelist Molly Ivins, a *Dallas Times Herald* columnist, former *Texas Observer* editor and liberal critic who gripes that the Legislature is controlled by business, engaged in a lively exchange with conservative Democratic state Rep. Bill Messer of Belton and Scott Bennett, a *Dallas Morning News* business-and-politics columnist.

Citing the low level of welfare payments the lawmakers set for needy children, Ivins said the Legislature's two most distinguishing characteristics are that it's "cheap and mean."

Agreeing with Messer that the Legislature is representative of Texas, Ivins said she also agreed with state Sen. Carl Parker, D-Port Arthur, that "if you took all the fools out of the Legislature, it would no longer be a representative body."

Messer, who has chaired the powerful House Calendars Committee for two regular sessions and subscribes to the maxim that "what's good for business is good for Texas," defended the Legislature's practice of favoring business.

The Legislature basically has always been representative of the people of Texas and has done what they wanted, said Messer, who soon will become a lobbyist.

Texas was populated by people who saw the state as a place of economic opportunity and wanted "a piece of the pie," he said. Therefore, they have elected majorities of legislators who "are basically business-oriented pragmatists, as opposed to social engineers or some others," he said.

Texans agree on about 95 per cent of what the state should do, and legislators reflect the agreement, he claimed.

For about four decades, the business and political establishments "worked together hand-in-glove" and lawmakers "felt like it was their job to help business every chance they could, and they did," Messer said. But this was what most Texans wanted, he claimed.

Even though there has been much change in the Legislature in recent decades, Messer contended the lawmakers are still doing what's good for business *and* Texas.

Columnist Bennett said it's "wonderful" that business has had "enormous impact on the evolution of Texas." Business has shown a high quality of leadership and has been dedicated to public policy serving the state's economic welfare, he said.

State Sen. Cyndi Taylor Krier, R-San Antonio, attributed the rapid growth of the Texas Republican Party to the increase in liberals in the Democratic Party, which has caused some conservatives to switch to the Republicans; the influx of new Texans from other states joining the GOP; the shift of population from traditionally Democratic rural areas to Republican-dominated urban areas; and the coming-of-age of new voters favoring the Republican Party.

"The battle for Texas political independence is won," Krier declared.

But liberal Ivins, who favored a two-party system, got in a dig at the GOP's rise.

"Whoever would have imagined that some people would start a political party to the right of the Texas Democratic Party?" she asked.

OTHER FORUM PARTICIPANTS

Felix D. Almaraz, Jr.
The University of Texas at San Antonio

Lynn F. Anderson
LBJ School of Public Affairs

Chris Kelly Andrews
Ultra Magazine

Peter Applebome
New York Times

Bill Arhos
KLRU-TV
Austin

Brux Austin
Texas Business Magazine

Donald Bacon
US News & World Report

Howard R. Balanoff
LBJ School of Public Affairs

Patricia Baldwin
Austin Business Journal

Douglas Barnett
Texas State Historical Association

Kit Bauman
Dallas Downtown News

Barbara B. Benavides
Davis & Smith
San Antonio

Garvin Berry
KTRH-AM & KPRC-TV
Houston

Kent Biffle
Dallas Morning News

Elizabeth Biondi
Vanity Fair

Terrell Blodgett
LBJ School of Public Affairs

Philip C. Bobbitt
The University of Texas at Austin

Cathy Bonner
Bonner, Inc.
Austin

Roland Boyd
Attorney
McKinney

Rose M. Brewer
The University of Texas at Austin

Phyllis Bridges
Texas Woman's University

Norman D. Brown
The University of Texas at Austin

Ronald M. Brown
The University of Texas at Austin

William D. Broyles, Sr.
W. D. Broyles & Associates
Houston

Alex Burton
KRLD-Radio
Dallas

Jacqueline Butler
Department of Human Services

J. Clifton Caldwell
Richardson

Randolph "Mike" Campbell
North Texas State University

Don E. Carleton
Barker Texas History Center

Christy Carpenter
Trintex
New York

Liz Carpenter
Writer
Austin

Chris Carson
Ford Powell & Carson Inc.
San Antonio

Gary Cartwright
Texas Monthly

Susan Chadwick
Writer
Houston

Jerome Chapman
Texas Health Care Association

Thomas L. Charlton
Baylor University

Richard K. Chen
Chinese Daily News
Houston

Charles B. Chick
Presidio Enterprises
Austin

Charles F. Cnudde
The University of Texas at Austin

Shelby Coffey III
Dallas Times Herald

Wilbur J. Cohen
LBJ School of Public Affairs

Robert Compton
Dallas Morning News

Martha Cotera
Austin Hispanic Directory

James L. Crowson
University of Texas System

William H. Cunningham
The University of Texas at Austin

Gregory Curtis
Texas Monthly

Thomas W. Cutrer
Texas State Historical Association

Carmina Danini
Laredo Morning News

Margaret Darden
Midwestern University

John Davidson
Texas Monthly

Jim Davis
Harte-Hanks Communications
Austin

Monica Davis
The Davis Group
Austin

Wilhelmina Delco
Texas House of Representatives

Robin Doughty
The University of Texas at Austin

Bill Douthat
Austin American-Statesman

Clif W. Drummond
Office of Governor Mark White

Ronnie Dugger
Texas Observer

Lyn Dunsavage
Dallas Downtown News

Roy J. Eaton
Wise County Messenger

Jane Ely
Houston Post

Howard Falkenberg
Staats Falkenberg & Partners, Inc.
Austin

Deborah Fant
Texas Monthly

Peggy Fikac
Freedom Newspapers-Valley

Laura Fisher
Texas Monthly

Nancy Fisher
Texas House of Representatives Staff

Dan Fleckman
Akin, Gump, Strauss, Hauer & Feld
Austin

Betty S. Flowers
The University of Texas at Austin

Raymond E. Frisbie
Texas A&M University

Robert K. German
LBJ School of Public Affairs

Lisa Germany
Writer
Eastland

Michael L. Gillette
LBJ Library

Robert L. Gillette
Attorney
Baytown

Don Graham
The University of Texas at Austin

A. C. Greene
Author
Dallas

George Norris Green
The University of Texas at Arlington

Katherine Gregor
Writer
Austin

Louis Grigar
Texas Education Agency

John A. Gronouski
LBJ School of Public Affairs

Jack Gullahorn
Attorney
Austin

Howard D. Gutin
KLRN-TV
San Antonio

Susan G. Hadden
LBJ School of Public Affairs

Elizabeth Hall
LBJ School of Public Affairs

Debbie Hanna
University of Houston

Robert L. Hardesty
Southwest Texas State University

Stephen Harrigan
Texas Monthly

Fred Hartman
Baytown Sun

Carol Hatfield
Discovery
The University of Texas at Austin

Tom Hatfield
The University of Texas at Austin

Bruce Hight
Austin American-Statesman

Rolando Hinojosa-Smith
The University of Texas at Austin

Bert Holmes
Dallas Times Herald

Michael Holmes
Associated Press

Wayne H. Holtzman
The University of Texas at Austin

David Humphrey
LBJ Library

Michael S. Hvezdos
Longview Newspapers, Inc.

Harold M. Hyman
Rice University

Jan Jarboe
San Antonio Express-News

Sharon Jayson
Texas State Network

Felicia Jeter
KHOU-TV
Houston

Jaclyn Lee Jeffrey
Baylor University

Robert C. Jeffrey
The University of Texas at Austin

Lady Bird Johnson
Austin

Nick Johnson
Bandera Bulletin

Jack Keever
Associated Press

Elmer Kelton
Livestock Weekly
San Angelo

Lorrin Kennamer
The University of Texas at Austin

Bill Kidd
Long News Service
Austin

Kathy Kiely
Houston Post

Sam Kinch, Jr.
Sam Kinch's Texas Weekly
Austin

John Q. Taylor King
Huston-Tillotson College

John Kings
Editor and Writer
Austin

Mike Kingston
Texas Almanac

Carole Kneeland
WFAA-TV
Austin

George Kozmetsky
The University of Texas at Austin

Thomas H. Kreneck
Houston Metropolitan Research Center

Joseph R. Krier
Grieshaber-Roberts, Inc.
San Antonio

Robert Krueger
LBJ School of Public Affairs

Tina Lawson
LBJ Library

Lowell Lebermann
Lebermann Investments
Austin

William S. Livingston
The University of Texas at Austin

Francis L. Loewenheim
Rice University

Susan Longley
State Comptroller's Office

Scott Lubeck
Texas Monthly Press

Thomas W. Luce III
Hughes & Luce
Dallas

Anna Macias
Dallas Morning News

Jack R. Maguire
Writer
Fredericksburg

David Maraniss
Washington Post

Ray Marshall
LBJ School of Public Affairs

Oscar J. Martinez
The University of Texas at El Paso

Maury Maverick, Jr.
Attorney
San Antonio

Gray McBride
RCS Investments
Dallas

Richard McCulley
LBJ School of Public Affairs

Archie P. McDonald
Stephen F. Austin State University

George McElroy
Houston Informer

Ross McSwain
San Angelo Standard-Times

Harry J. Middleton
LBJ Library

Cathy Mincberg
Houston Independent School District

Stephen A. Monti
The University of Texas at Austin

John Moore
State Comptroller's Office

Karen Mosman
Sesquicentennial Commission

Ruben Munguia
Munguia Printers, Inc.
San Antonio

Joe Murray
The Lufkin Daily News

Vance Muse
Writer
New York

Garry L. Nall
West Texas State University

Kaye Northcott
Writer
Austin

John Odam
Attorney
Houston

Peggy Odam
Houston

Howard T. Odum
LBJ School of Public Affairs

Roger M. Olien
University of Texas at the Permian Basin

Shirley Bird Perry
The University of Texas at Austin

Jake Pickle
U.S. Congress

Dudley L. Poston
The University of Texas at Austin

Pike Powers
Attorney
Austin

J. Mike Quinn
The University of Texas at Austin

Clinton Rabb
McKinley Avenue
Methodist Church
San Antonio

Kenneth B. Ragsdale
Writer
Austin

Audray Bateman Randle
Austin History Center

Dick Rathgeber
Developer
Austin

Shannon H. Ratliff
The University of Texas at Austin

Dick J. Reavis
Texas Monthly

Emmette S. Redford
LBJ School of Public Affairs

Jan Reid
Texas Monthly

Dale Rice
Dallas Times Herald

Walter H. Richter
Former State Senator
Austin

Robert C. Rickards
LBJ School of Public Affairs

Geoffrey Rips
Texas Observer

Clay Robison
Houston Chronicle

Bob Rogers
Bryan-College Station Eagle

Ricardo Romo
The University of Texas at Austin

Karl C. Rove
Karl Rove & Company
Austin

Linda Scarbrough
Williamson County Sun

Frances Schenkkan
Austin Planning Commission

Richard Schott
LBJ School of Public Affairs

Richard Seaman
Abilene Reporter-News

Edwin R. Sharpe
The University of Texas at Austin

Patricia Sharpe
Texas Monthly

Rebecca Sharpless
Baylor University

Gene Alice Sherman
Texas Committee for the Humanities
Austin

Max Sherman
LBJ School of Public Affairs

Ted Siff
Quorum Report

Ed Sills
San Antonio Light

Ada Simond
W. H. Passon Historical Society
Austin

Mark Singer
The New Yorker Magazine

Ernest T. Smerdon
The University of Texas at Austin

Martha Smiley
Bickerstaff, Heath & Smiley
Austin

C. B. Smith, Sr.
C. B. Smith Investments
Austin

Glenn Smith
Houston Post

Thomas J. Smith
Davis & Smith
San Antonio

William G. Smith
Texas Business Magazine

Neal Spelce
Neal Spelce Communications
Austin

Stephen H. Spurr
LBJ School of Public Affairs

William J. Strickler
The University of Texas at Austin

Mimi Swartz
Texas Monthly

Helen Tackett
University of Texas News and
Information Service

John Taliaferro
Third Coast Magazine

Ellen Temple
Texas Foundation for Women's Resources

Larry Temple
Coordinating Board, Texas College and
University System

Marshall Terry
Southern Methodist University

Patrick Terry
Sesquicentennial Commission

Kyle Thompson
Fort Worth Star-Telegram

Saralee Tiede
Office of the Lieutenant Governor

Robert Tissing
LBJ Library

Terry Toler
Austin Homes and Gardens Magazine

Richard J. Trabulsi, Jr.
Attorney
Houston

Laura Tuma
Austin Magazine

Curtis Tunnell
Texas Historical Commission

Steven Van
Prism Hotel Development Company
Dallas

Olivia Walker
Texas Senate Staff

Bill Walraven
Corpus Christi Caller

Charles Worth Ward
Wichita Falls Times & Record News

George B. Ward
Texas State Historical Association

John Edward Weems
Writer
Waco

Sidney Weintraub
LBJ School of Public Affairs

Felton West
Houston Post

Richard West
D Magazine

Judith Wilkerson
Pleasanton Express

Frederick Williams
The University of Texas at Austin

Jerre S. Williams
United States Circuit Judge
Austin

Mary Pearl Williams
53rd District Court Judge
Austin

Stephanie Williams
KTBC-TV
Austin

Gary C. Wilson
Texas Monthly

Robert H. Wilson
LBJ School of Public Affairs

Will Wilson, Sr.
Attorney
Austin

Dorman Winfrey
Texas State Library

Fritz Wirt
The Huntsville Item

Sally Wittliff
Urban Design Task Force
Austin

Warren G. Woodward
Bass Brothers Enterprises, Inc.
Fort Worth

George C. Wright
The University of Texas at Austin

Lawrence Wright
Texas Monthly

Gary Yarrington
LBJ Library

Emily Yoffe
Texas Monthly

Terry Young
Read Poland Associates
Austin

Richard Zelade
Texas Monthly